HOME DESIGN WORKBOOKS
HOME
OFFICE

HOME DESIGN WORKBOOKS

HOME OFFICE

SARAH GAVENTA

DORLING KINDERSLEY
LONDON • NEW YORK • SYDNEY • MOSCOW

A DORLING KINDERSLEY BOOK

Project Editor SUSIE BEHAR
Project Art Editor MARTIN LOVELOCK
DTP Designer MARK BRACEY
Photography PETER ANDERSON, ANDY CRAWFORD
Stylist EMILY HEDGES
Production Controller MICHELLE THOMAS
Series Editor CHARLOTTE DAVIES
Series Art Editor CLIVE HAYBALL

First published in Great Britain in 1998 by
Dorling Kindersley Limited
9 Henrietta Street, London WC2E 8PS

A CIP catalogue record for this book
is available from the British Library

ISBN 0 7513 0469 7

Text film output in Great Britain by R & B Creative Services Ltd.
Reproduced in Singapore by Pica
Printed in Great Britain by Butler & Tanner Ltd., Frome and London

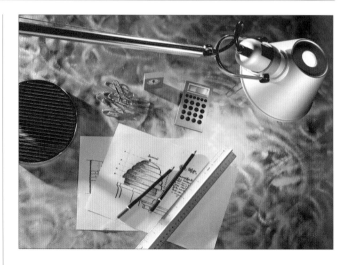

INTRODUCTION · 6

HOME OFFICE ELEMENTS · 20

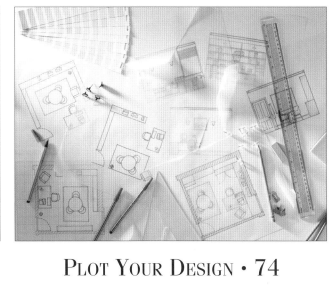

ROOM PLANS · 48

PLOT YOUR DESIGN · 74

CONTENTS

INTRODUCTION

OUTDOOR OFFICE △ ▽
For George Bernard Shaw, the Irish dramatist, this simple summer house served as a secluded home office where he was freed from distraction and able to make the most of fresh air and fine weather.

Working from home is not a new phenomenon: it is, of course, the original work environment, having evolved from the artist's studio, the man of letter's study, the scholar's library, and the writer's den. Looking at some famous examples of historical home offices may provide inspiration for your own. One of my favourites is Vita Sackville West's library/writing room in a tower at her home in Sissinghurst, Kent, with fine views of her famous garden, pale walls, kelim-strewn floors, and books everywhere in handy reach of her chair. A simpler, less-cluttered favourite is Ernest Hemingway's retreat in Cuba – a separate writing tower next to his villa in San Francisco de Paula, Cuba – where he could climb up to work in a single room containing only a wooden chair, desk, telescope, mug of pencils, and a few hunting trophies. The Irish dramatist George Bernard Shaw's summer house (*see left*) is also simple, apart from an ingenious rotating mechanism under the floor, which allowed the writer to enjoy all-day sunshine.

But working from home is no longer just a dream that can be realized only by the talented few. A combination of new technology and rationalization of working practices, along with demands for a better quality of life, means that more and more people work from home; recent estimates suggest that worldwide, the figure is around 40 million and growing.

CHANGING WORK PRACTICES

As the nature of work changes, the nine-to-five "battery chicken" approach to working in commercial offices has, for many, become outmoded. In any case "jobs for life" are no longer guaranteed, nor even desired; short-term contracts are commonplace, and many people expect to have a number of jobs over their working life. Many companies now contract out their services, employing consultants instead of full-time staff to provide specialist skills. These consultancies are often one-person set-ups that can be operated successfully from home. A growing number of companies, inspired by the increasing sophistication of computer and communication systems, have come to realize the value of teleworking, allowing staff to work

◁ **INDIVIDUAL STYLE**
Colour, pattern, personal objects, and domestic-style furniture combine to create an informal and stimulating work environment that is far removed from the standard commercial office.

either full or part time at home, and to keep in touch with the parent company by computer and telephone links. Organizations now exist to give advice on teleworking.

Working at home is not merely a business decision but an important lifestyle choice. It can radically transform the way you work, the way you spend your leisure time, and how you view your home. For large numbers of workers who have to combine work with bringing up children, it provides a flexible and manageable solution to childminding problems.

Current research shows that for some people, work is no longer the be-all and end-all of life. There has been a change in priorities for many of today's workers, who believe there is little

point in working twelve hours a day, six days a week if you are too tired or have no spare time to enjoy spending the money you earn. Home working, however, can fit in with other areas of your life, such as family commitments and entertaining friends, allowing you greater flexibility and the freedom to work from 6pm to 6am, or in your pyjamas, if that is how and when you are most productive.

The increase in severe cases of stress, repetitive strain injury, and so-called "sick-building syndrome" – all modern afflictions associated with unhealthy office environments – have resulted in the health-conscious worker demanding a work environment that respects the user and is as pleasant and stress-free as possible.

ABOUT YOU

Consider these basic questions relating to your personality to help you create a successful method of home working and a suitable home office environment.

☐ Are you used to a sociable office? Do you find other people's input stimulating? If so, when working at home, would you enjoy sharing your office?

☐ Are you a tidy worker? Do you clear your desk when you stop work? Or, do you need to screen off your office area after work?

☐ Are you easily distracted by other people, household chores, or phone conversations with friends? If so, would working in total privacy, away from intrusive phonecalls, be helpful?

☐ Do you plan to set formal hours for working, such as 9am to 5pm, or would you prefer more flexible hours? Do you have the self-discipline to work irregular hours?

And the conditions people are demanding in the office can often be most easily satisfied at home.

A well-designed home office is the ultimate expression of personal choice, embodying the power to create an environment that is specially designed to meet your individual needs, idiosyncrasies, and tastes. It can provide all the facilities of a commercial office plus the many advantages of being at home, such as choice of decor and colour scheme, good natural light, comfort, and personal control.

THE ROLE OF ERGONOMICS

Your home office should be designed with practicality as well as comfort in mind. The perfect environment to aid creativity and productivity requires careful planning and analysis – in other words it needs to be designed ergonomically. Ergonomics is the study of the relationship between workers and their environment, particularly the equipment they use. In practice, it means choosing the right desk and chair and positioning furniture and equipment to maximize efficiency and minimize physical effort and discomfort.

By considering your work patterns and requirements before making any decisions, you will not only save yourself needless time and expense but, more importantly, you will avoid strain and injury from using badly designed or incorrectly positioned products. Think about how you work, how long you spend at your desk, how often you go out, and what items you need around you. Think, too, about how long you will spend working at home. What are your

priorities in terms of furniture and equipment, and what can you afford to spend? Look at other offices and notice what you like and dislike about them. Borrow ideas and inspiration from others, look in magazines and catalogues to see what is new, and, just as importantly, examine your home carefully to see whether any existing items of furniture can be adapted for office use.

WHERE IN THE HOME?

Choosing the right space to convert into your home office is important. If you plan to work full time at home, then most of your day will be spent there, so choose a space that can be made attractive and welcoming, not some dank, dark area that is inadequate for any other function. The space you choose may be dictated by your work needs: for example, illustrators and designers prefer good, even light, so a loft space or rear extension with ample natural light would be ideal. On the other hand, if your work

△ MODULAR STORAGE
Work files and storage need
not be dull and messy. The
availability of colourful
folders and box files, and
of stylish, modular storage
units like these, ensures that
filing can be kept both neat
and attractive.

MOBILE STORAGE ▷
Look for functional products that retain a domestic scale and finish, such as this blue plastic trolley with four storage drawers.

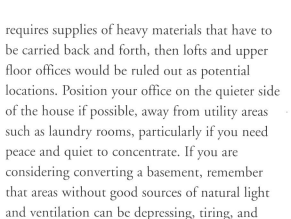

requires supplies of heavy materials that have to be carried back and forth, then lofts and upper floor offices would be ruled out as potential locations. Position your office on the quieter side of the house if possible, away from utility areas such as laundry rooms, particularly if you need peace and quiet to concentrate. If you are considering converting a basement, remember that areas without good sources of natural light and ventilation can be depressing, tiring, and

unhealthy to work in. Views can be either inspiring or distracting: looking out onto a busy street scene may make concentration difficult and turn you into a nosey neighbour.

Employing others at home can bring additional problems. Check local regulations about the number of people who can work in your home before health and safety regulations come into force. Think, too, about whether you would find it irksome to have colleagues traipsing through

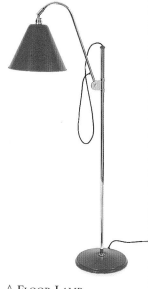

△ **FLOOR LAMP**
An adjustable floor lamp provides a good source of task lighting without taking up valuable desk space. It must have a heavy base to ensure stability.

WHAT DO YOU WANT FROM YOUR OFFICE?

Before committing yourself to expensive furniture and equipment, analyze your work patterns and lifestyle and how you intend to use your new office. To help you decide what will work best for you, consider the benefits of the work spaces shown below.

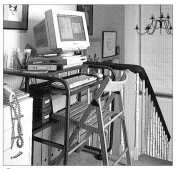

❶ LIGHT AND VIEWS

❷ WARMTH AND DOMESTICITY

❸ SIMPLICITY

❹ MOBILITY AND FLEXIBILITY

❺ ABILITY TO CONCEAL

❻ ORDER AND EFFICIENCY

△ ADAPTABLE STORAGE
Fibreboard storage boxes, such as these, provide a flexible, hardwearing, yet inexpensive storage system for your home office. The boxes, in a range of sizes, can be bought individually and stacked to allow for expanding needs.

THE RIGHT CHAIR ▷
Ergonomic consideration is vital in both your choice of task chair and in ensuring that it is positioned correctly to support your lumbar region and prevent backache. The chair should move with you as you move, whether you are leaning forwards over your desk, or leaning back to stretch tired limbs.

your home, and bear this in mind when deciding where to set up your office. Remember, too, that if co-workers want to get into work early, you will probably want to be up and dressed – a constraint that may detract from the freedom of working from home.

HOME-WORKING PSYCHOLOGY

Creating the correct environment is essential, but so too is developing the right attitude towards working at home. For those who have gone from working five days a week in a frenetic open-plan office, surrounded by colleagues, suddenly being on one's own can come as a shock. Most home workers admit to finding the lack of social interaction difficult, and cite this as the main drawback to working at home. Many break up their day by visiting clients, shopping, or playing sports, which bring them into contact with other people. Some have even set up networks with other home workers whom they can meet regularly during the daytime.

Although the telephone or e-mail is not always an adequate substitute for direct human contact, most home workers spend more time on the phone than other workers, partly through the need to talk to someone. Friends, who wouldn't dream of disturbing you if you were at work in a commercial office, feel that they can call you at anytime when they know you work at home, thereby creating distractions and loss of concentration. A separate business telephone line can help, as can urging your friends to leave you in peace during office hours.

Starting work each day can be the hardest part. A friend of mine can begin working in his home office only if he dresses in formal office clothes, leaves the house at a regular time, walks round to the back door, and then heads for his home office. An extreme example perhaps, but getting into the right frame of mind and being disciplined is vital when you work at home.

Keeping your home office sacrosanct can help, for example by banning family members and demanding pets during office hours. There are endless distractions at home so, if you know that you lack self discipline, make sure that you keep possible temptations out of sight.

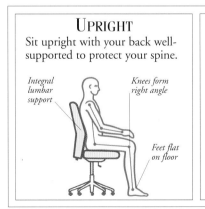

UPRIGHT
Sit upright with your back well-supported to protect your spine.

Integral lumbar support
Knees form right angle
Feet flat on floor

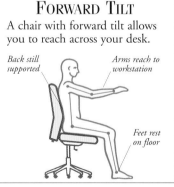

FORWARD TILT
A chair with forward tilt allows you to reach across your desk.

Back still supported
Arms reach to workstation
Feet rest on floor

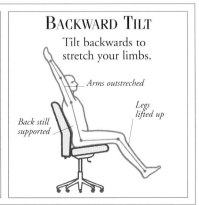

BACKWARD TILT
Tilt backwards to stretch your limbs.

Arms outstreched
Back still supported
Legs lifted up

◁ **STABLE CONVERSION**
A former stable has been transformed into a delightful, light and airy studio space. The original tethering post has been retained, adding to the studio's character.

The temptation to keep working, when time is money, can be overwhelming. But being able to work anytime should not mean that you work all the time. Learning to switch off can be difficult, especially if your carefully designed home office is such a wonderful space that you don't want to leave it. Some home workers set themselves a maximum number of working hours per day. Some stop when a partner who works elsewhere returns home. Don't become a slave to your home office, it should help you to work more efficiently and create more time for other activities. If one of your reasons for setting up a home office is to spend more time with your family, remember not to equate working at home with being at home. Avoid arranging meetings in the evenings, and anything else that will interfere with your home life routine. It is very important to know when to switch off.

Everybody has their own way of working and only you can decide what your needs are and what works best for you. The French novelist, Marcel Proust, used to work in a room with the shutters closed and the curtains drawn – but not everyone has to go to such lengths to work effectively at home. In this book, we concentrate on the practical factors that you need to consider when setting up a home office, and suggest general pointers that might help you to work more efficiently, happily, and safely.

CHOOSING YOUR OFFICE STYLE

Part of the fun is deciding how you want your office to look, especially as there is no need to recreate the look of a commercial office. Consider carefully the style and type of furniture you need, bearing in mind that you may be working and living with it for a considerable time to come. Plan where everything is to go before indulging in a spending spree. If your budget is limited, check around your home for little-used items that can be recycled into your

△ **STACKING STOOLS**
Spare seating taken from elsewhere in your home, such as these stacking stools, can double as temporary seating when clients or colleagues visit your office.

TUB CHAIR ▷
Compact and comfortable, this tub chair, upholstered in bright red leather, provides ideal seating for a relaxed business meeting.

office, such as kitchen chairs for meeting chairs, bedside lamps for ambient lighting, or a music-centre as a printer or fax stand. Visit local junk shops and second-hand office furniture suppliers: respraying or reupholstering will transform your bargains. Select your colour scheme, integrating items such as files, furniture, and accessories to create a pleasing, coordinated office. Invest in extra files of the same type to maintain the look of your office in case they are discontinued. And remember: home working is a positive lifestyle

choice, offering freedom to control your working environment and flexibility in how you work. Appreciate planning a home office that is tailormade just for you, one that reflects your style and personality and caters for your specific work requirements as well as fitting in with your other commitments. Pamper yourself with at least one luxury item, be it a leather chair or espresso machine. And don't rush decisions, you may be working with the results for a long time. Enjoy the process, it is an exciting challenge.

INTEGRATED OFFICE ▽
A modern, open-plan flat offers the opportunity to create a home office that is integrated into the main living space, while still providing partial visual separation and privacy.

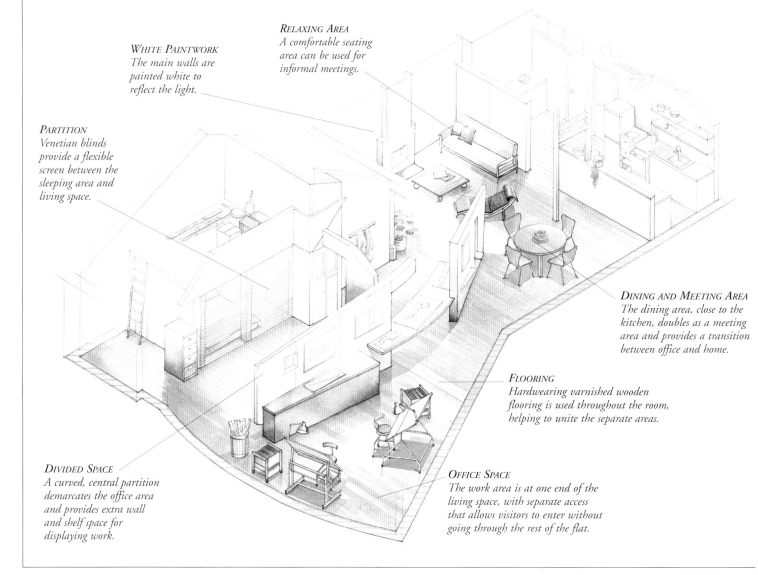

WHITE PAINTWORK
The main walls are painted white to reflect the light.

RELAXING AREA
A comfortable seating area can be used for informal meetings.

PARTITION
Venetian blinds provide a flexible screen between the sleeping area and living space.

DINING AND MEETING AREA
The dining area, close to the kitchen, doubles as a meeting area and provides a transition between office and home.

FLOORING
Hardwearing varnished wooden flooring is used throughout the room, helping to unite the separate areas.

DIVIDED SPACE
A curved, central partition demarcates the office area and provides extra wall and shelf space for displaying work.

OFFICE SPACE
The work area is at one end of the living space, with separate access that allows visitors to enter without going through the rest of the flat.

PLAN OF ACTION

Before starting on any alterations, use this checklist to make sure that you have not over-looked any important requirements. If you plan to convert part of your home into an office, you will have to coordinate the work of architects, builders, and electricians.

☐ Have you received permission from the relevant authorities for structural alterations?
☐ Will you need professional help to convert your office?
☐ Have you estimated costs correctly and checked that delivery dates will allow you to have a fully functional office from the start?
☐ If your budget is tight, could you build a desk rather than buy a ready-made one?
☐ Is your design flexible enough to allow for adaptation and growth?
☐ Will your alterations detract from the value of your property?
☐ Can you work somewhere else while building is in progress?

◁ **TRADITIONAL STYLE**
If you do not require a lot of equipment, a traditional study area may be sufficient. In this comfortable space, books and files are concealed behind simple drapes.

HOW THIS BOOK WORKS

THIS BOOK gives you the practical know-how you need to design an office that matches your lifestyle, and create an efficient and comfortable work space; it will help you plan a brand-new office or adapt a living space. A series of questions helps you assess what you need from your office, then a survey of furniture and fittings helps you to choose the right elements for your work space. Next, three-dimensional plans of six offices explain how to engineer a successful design, and finally, instructions on measuring and drawing up an office plan leave you equipped to translate ideas into reality.

2. SELECT FITTINGS ▽

To help you compile a list of the features that will best suit your requirements, a range of furniture, fittings, and equipment are surveyed (pp.20–47). A "Remember" box draws your attention to important design points, and the advantages and disadvantages of each element are assessed. Simple diagrams demonstrate where in the room to position your furniture and equipment for maximum safety, comfort, and efficiency.

1. IDENTIFY YOUR NEEDS ▽

A number of preliminary questions (pp.16–19) are asked to encourage you to think about your office needs, and the suitability and potential of your choice of room. By examining aspects of your personal and professional life, such as how you work, relax, and entertain, you will find it easier to identify the most suitable equipment and most appropriate design solutions for adapting a room or building a new office.

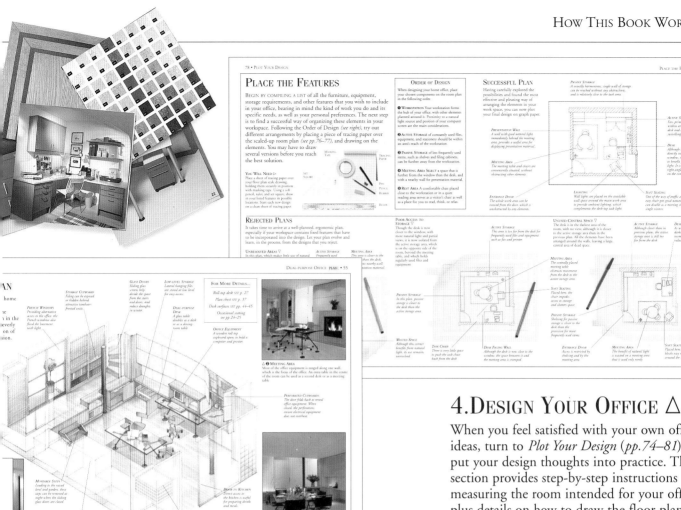

4. DESIGN YOUR OFFICE △

When you feel satisfied with your own office ideas, turn to *Plot Your Design* (*pp.74–81*), and put your design thoughts into practice. This section provides step-by-step instructions for measuring the room intended for your office, plus details on how to draw the floor plan and different wall elevations to scale. Common design mistakes are pinpointed and successful solutions are shown and explained.

3. LEARN HOW TO PLAN △

A chapter on *Room Plans* (*pp.48–73*) looks in detail at six existing office designs and offers advice and inspiration on how to bring together all the elements in your own plan. A three-dimensional drawing, a bird's eye view plan, photographs, and a list of design points explain the thinking behind each design solution.

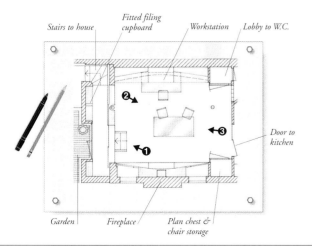

Stairs to house

Fitted filing cupboard

Workstation

Lobby to W.C.

Door to kitchen

Garden

Fireplace

Plan chest & chair storage

HOW TO USE THE GRAPH PAPER

■ Draw up your room to scale (*see pp.76–77*) using the graph paper provided (*pp.89–96*). You may photocopy it if you need more.

■ For an office with small dimensions, use the graph paper with a metric scale of 1:20, where one large square represents 1m and one small square represents 10cm. Therefore, an area 60cm long is drawn as six small squares. Alternatively, use the imperial scale of 1:24, where one large square represents 1ft and a small square 3in.

■ For a larger office, use the graph paper with the smaller scale of 1:50. The large squares represent 1m and the small squares 10cm. Or, use the imperial graph paper with the scale of 1:48, where a large square equals 4ft and a small square 6in.

■ Having plotted your room, try various designs on a tracing paper overlay.

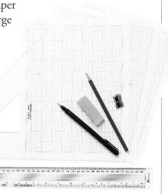

ASSESS YOUR NEEDS

THE FOLLOWING QUESTIONS will help you to focus on the major issues affecting where you place your home office, how you furnish it, what equipment you require, and the type of office environment that best suits you and your lifestyle.

FURNITURE

Investing in well-designed office furniture is vital for a safe and comfortable working environment. Your starting point should be the choice of task chair – the most important tool in your office.

■ SEATING

☐ Do you spend more than two hours every day seated at your desk? If so, have you budgeted for an ergonomic chair?
☐ If you intend to employ people to work in your home office, have you checked office seating regulations?
☐ Do you suffer from backache? If you do, have you considered a chair with specialist back support?
☐ Do you require extra seating for clients and meetings, or could you use your dining-room or kitchen chairs?
☐ Will you need to seat clients or guests for long periods of time, or will stacking chairs or stools be adequate?
☐ Do you need to store away your chair after work? If so, is it sufficiently mobile to be easily moved?
☐ Have you investigated which type of task chair castor will best suit the flooring in your office?

■ WORKSTATIONS

☐ Do you have a special routine or method of working that requires expansive worksurfaces for planning, organization, reference, and layout?
☐ Can you use or adapt an existing piece of furniture, such as a dining-room table for your desk, or do your require a specially designed worksurface?
☐ Do you require constant access to storage and reference material from your workstation? If so, do you want your worktop linked to storage facilities?
☐ Would you prefer a fitted workstation or do you want the flexibility of a freestanding desk?

☐ If you want to easily conceal your workstation, would you prefer a complete, closeable office unit or to section off your work area behind a screen?
☐ If your home office is situated in a living area, would a mobile desk be useful?
☐ If you need a large work area, would an L-shaped desk with a return be helpful?
☐ If you use a laptop, do you actually need a fixed workstation?

■ SURFACES AND FINISHES

☐ Does your type of work require a particularly hardwearing worksurface?
☐ Is the existing floor covering suitable for office furniture? If the room is carpeted, is the pile too thick for castors to work properly?
☐ Does the floor covering provide a measure of acoustic control?
☐ If you are working with electrical equipment, have you considered a non-static floor covering?
☐ Do you want all your surface finishes to coordinate, for example, to match wooden floors with a wooden desk?

MEETING AREAS

Think about the type of meeting area you require: formal or informal, permanent or temporary, large or small. How frequently will you receive visiting clients or colleagues? Will you regularly be meeting more than one person at a time?

☐ Have you considered the type of impression you want to make on clients or visitors, for example, informal and creative or business-like?
☐ How many people will be working in your office or visiting on a regular basis? If you are going to have frequent visitors, have you considered what facilities you would like to offer?
☐ Is it important to you that your meetings do not intrude on your home life and vice versa?
☐ Do you have the space for a dedicated meeting area, or do you need to adapt other rooms in the house, such as the kitchen or dining room?
☐ Do you want easy access to amenities, such as coffee- or tea-making facilities or the telephone, during meetings?
☐ Would it be useful to create a waiting area for visitors?
☐ Do you require additional space and specialist equipment for displays and presentations?

STORAGE

Think about your present storage requirements, and how much material you will accumulate over six months, then over a year. Work out which items you use frequently, which you use only occasionally, and which you can place in archive storage.

☐ Are there files and equipment that you use every day that need to be close to your workstation? Are there any heavy or large items that you can successfully store out of reach?
☐ Would you prefer your stored items to be visible or concealed?
☐ Do you require secure storage for valuable goods or cash?
☐ Does your regular work involve storing over-sized items, such as plans?
☐ Do you work with many documents that need long-term storage? Have you planned for archive storage space?
☐ Do you require secure archive storage or would wooden or cardboard boxes be sufficient for your needs?
☐ Have you specific paper size requirements which would affect your choice of storage systems?
☐ Do you need fireproof storage for precious files?
☐ Are there some items you would prefer to hide behind closed doors?

LIGHTING

Correct levels of lighting while you work help to reduce eyestrain, headaches, and fatigue. Your lighting requirements vary according to the type of work involved, and the quality and quantity of natural light the office receives. Office outlook will also have a bearing on how the room is best lit.

☐ When making your choice of work area, have you thought about whether you prefer natural or artificial lighting?
☐ Is the quality of natural light in the room good, or should you consider adding a window? Would a new window raise the level of natural light without taking away valuable wall space?
☐ Can you position your desk to take advantage of natural light while avoiding glare on your computer screen?
☐ Is it important that your work area is well-lit with task lamps?
☐ Would your environment be improved by atmospheric lighting?
☐ Are you short of floor space? Have you considered desk and wall lamps?
☐ Do you need to simulate daylight for your work?
☐ Have you considered using low-energy lamps to save energy?
☐ Could painting the room in a light colour make more of the available natural light?
☐ Would blinds help you to control sunlight shining in your eyes?

TECHNOLOGY

Although it it advisable to consult a specialist about your information technology requirements, consider beforehand some basic questions about space availability, electricity supply, ventilation, and safety.

☐ What office equipment will you need? Will your requirements change?
☐ Do you have the space for large office machines, such as photocopiers?
☐ Before you place your furniture, have you considered your cabling needs?
☐ Have you positioned regularly used equipment close to your workstation?
☐ Does noise bother you? Is there space to house noisy equipment away from your workstation?
☐ Would it be helpful to combine information technology, such as a joint fax and photocopier, to save space?
☐ Have you considered the heat build up from your equipment and planned to install proper ventilation?

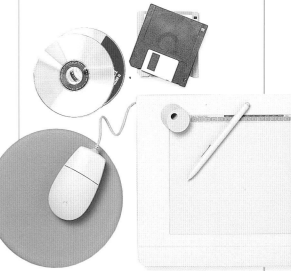

PERSONALIZING YOUR SPACE

Working at home gives you the opportunity to personalize your space in a way that working in a commercial office does not allow. Make a list of the luxuries you would like to have around you at work. But take into account how this environment will affect your attitude to work.

☐ Do you want to bring your home into your office or do you want to create a distinct office environment?
☐ Would you like your office to reflect your personality or to remain neutral?
☐ Do you prefer working in an informal or formal atmosphere?
☐ Do you feel at home with a particular style of decor and furniture?
☐ If your office is part of a shared living area, do you want the office decor to match the style?
☐ Have you considered which colours you find relaxing and calming, and which you find stimulating?
☐ If you have children, would you enjoy being able to see or hear them while you are working?
☐ If you have pets, do you want them around you while you work?

SPACE AND ACCESS

When choosing a room or area for your office, assess its accessibility to the exterior for receiving letters, goods, and visitors, and the level of security. Access to and from your office to the rest of the house, the kitchen, and the garden is also crucial. Estimate how much space you need to fulfil your basic requirements.

☐ Is the total space big enough for your needs? Have you chosen an area that can be extended?
☐ Is there a particular part of your home to which you would like your office to be linked, such as the kitchen, garden, or living room?
☐ Is there easy access to the front door for clients and to receive deliveries?
☐ If space is limited, can you remove architectural features, such as fireplaces, to create more room?
☐ Do you plan to install expensive equipment? If so, have you worked out security precautions?
☐ Will clients have to walk through the house to reach the office? If so, is this a problem in terms of domestic privacy?
☐ Do you value quiet while you work? Is this more important than having easy access to other areas of the house?

WHERE IN THE HOME?

Your office can be successfully situated in most rooms or areas of your home; it can occupy part of a living area, have its own room, or be situated in an outbuilding. If you answer yes to several or all the questions in a particular group below, the space described may be the most appropriate one for your working needs.

■ **DEDICATED ROOM**
☐ Do you require privacy from other household members?
☐ Do you use noisy equipment?
☐ Will you be holding regular meetings or frequently using the telephone?
☐ Do you require extensive storage space for files and equipment?

■ **SHARED LIVING AND OFFICE SPACE**
☐ Is your work part-time?
☐ Do you enjoy working in the company of other family members?
☐ Do you have the house to yourself during the day?
☐ Do you have limited equipment and storage needs?

■ **DUAL-PURPOSE ROOM**
☐ Do you have a room that you use only occasionally, such as a guest bedroom or a formal dining room?
☐ Is your need for office space only occasional?

■ **OUTBUILDING**
☐ Would you enjoy complete privacy while you work?
☐ Does your work involve using noisy equipment?
☐ Have you considered the cost and possible problems involved in installing heating, and power and telephone points?
☐ Have you thought about how to make the outbuilding secure?

WHICH ROOM?

Decide on the type of office or work space that best suits your needs, such as a dedicated room or shared living and office space. Then weigh up the advantages and disadvantages of each area, bearing in mind considerations such as the amount of natural light, privacy, and ease of access.

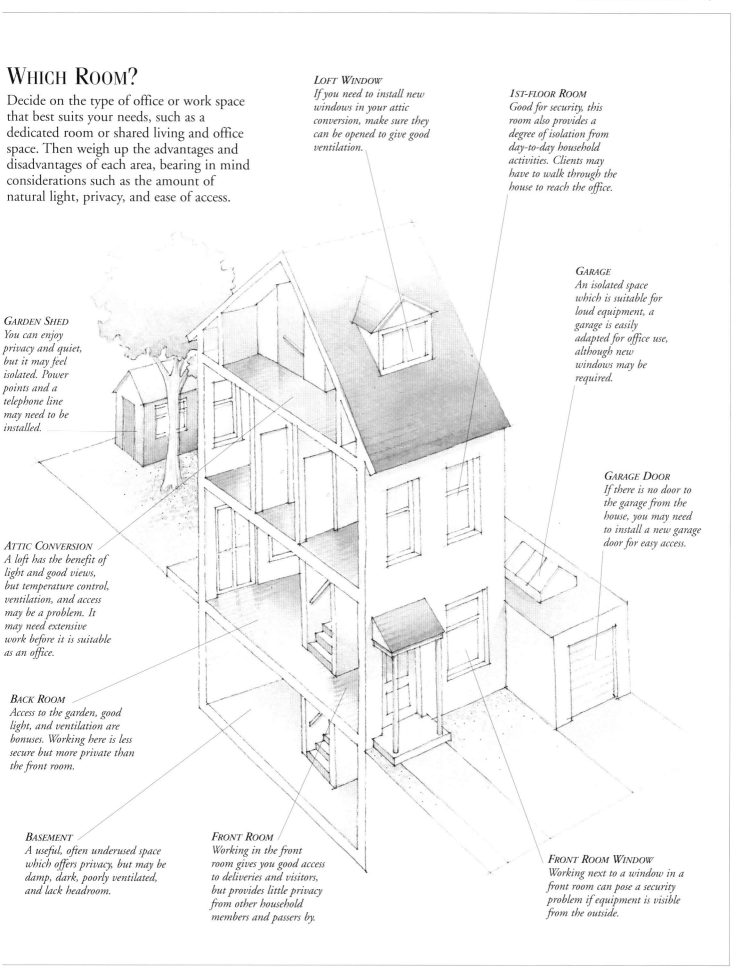

LOFT WINDOW
If you need to install new windows in your attic conversion, make sure they can be opened to give good ventilation.

1ST-FLOOR ROOM
Good for security, this room also provides a degree of isolation from day-to-day household activities. Clients may have to walk through the house to reach the office.

GARAGE
An isolated space which is suitable for loud equipment, a garage is easily adapted for office use, although new windows may be required.

GARDEN SHED
You can enjoy privacy and quiet, but it may feel isolated. Power points and a telephone line may need to be installed.

GARAGE DOOR
If there is no door to the garage from the house, you may need to install a new garage door for easy access.

ATTIC CONVERSION
A loft has the benefit of light and good views, but temperature control, ventilation, and access may be a problem. It may need extensive work before it is suitable as an office.

BACK ROOM
Access to the garden, good light, and ventilation are bonuses. Working here is less secure but more private than the front room.

BASEMENT
A useful, often underused space which offers privacy, but may be damp, dark, poorly ventilated, and lack headroom.

FRONT ROOM
Working in the front room gives you good access to deliveries and visitors, but provides little privacy from other household members and passers by.

FRONT ROOM WINDOW
Working next to a window in a front room can pose a security problem if equipment is visible from the outside.

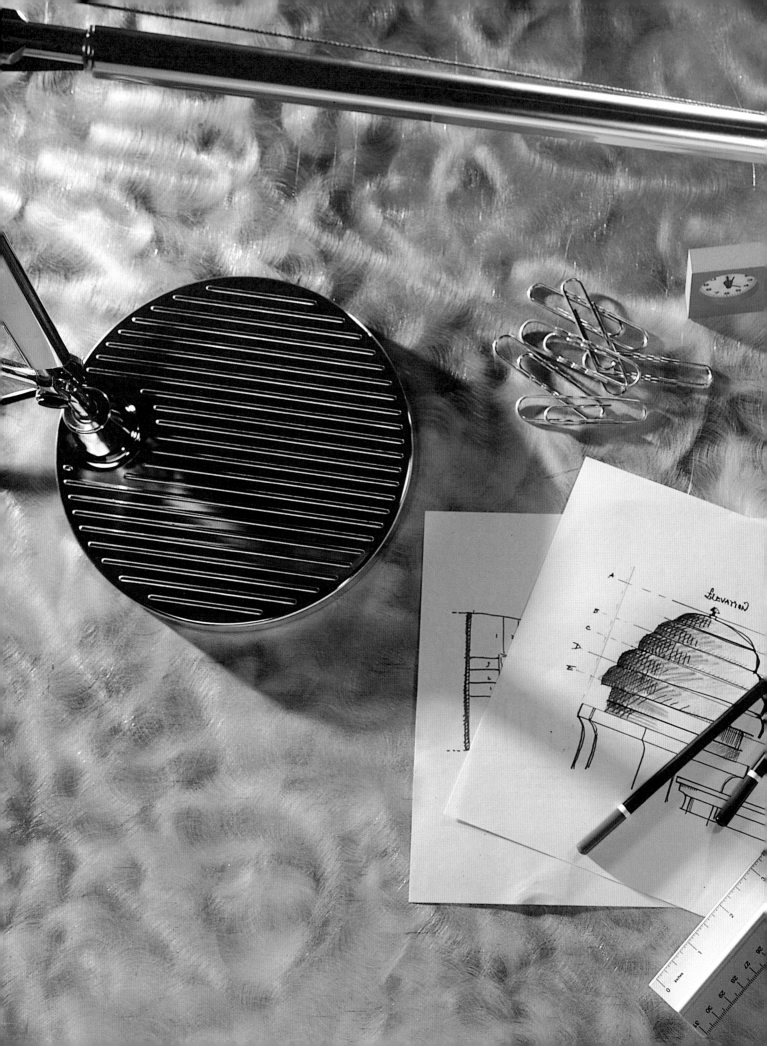

HOME OFFICE ELEMENTS

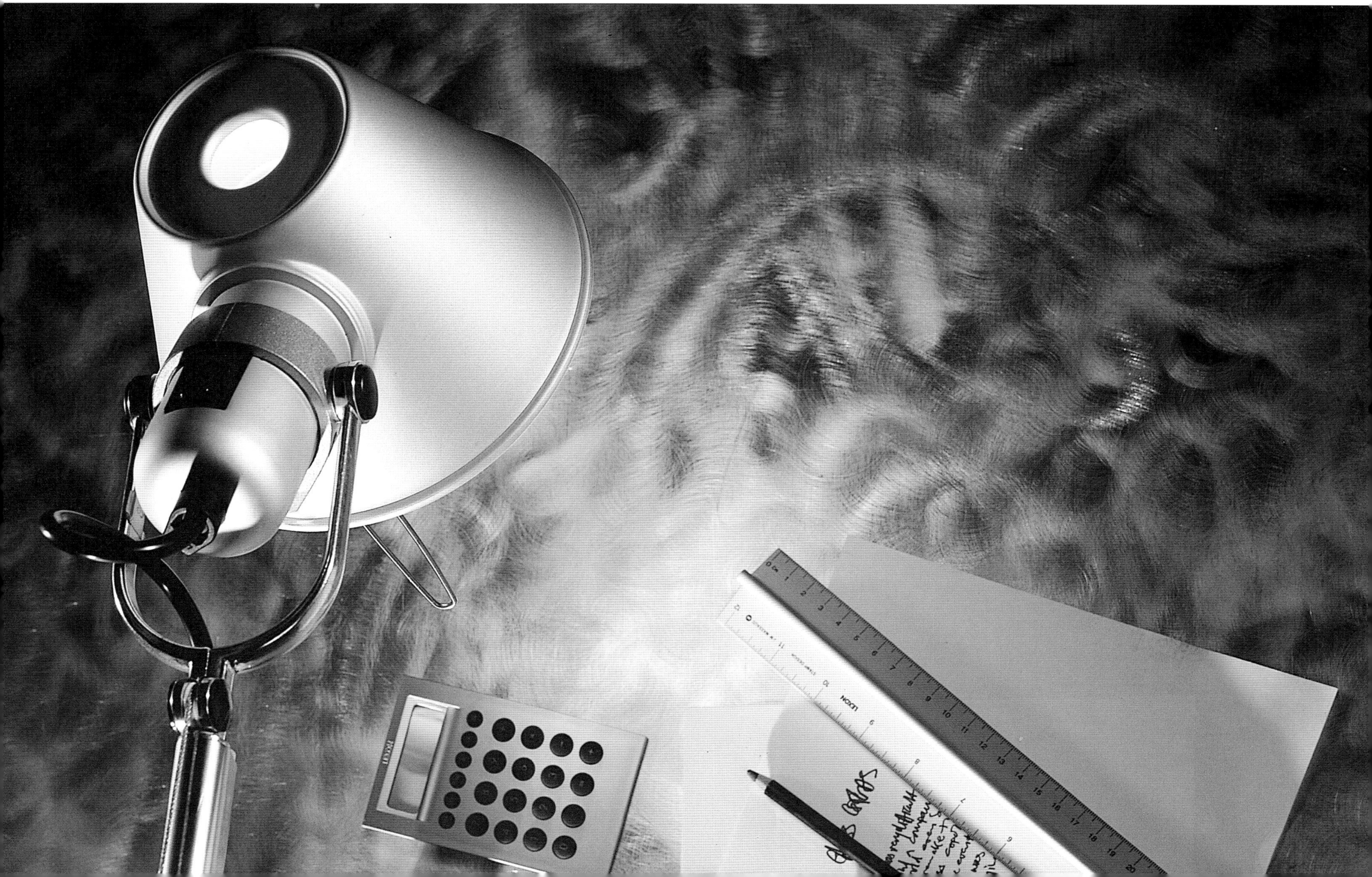

LONG-TERM SEATING

YOUR WORK OR TASK CHAIR is, in many ways, the most important piece of equipment in your home office. Prolonged use of an inadequate chair can result in backache, fatigue, and stress injury. Investment in a good-quality, ergonomically designed chair is essential for your health and productivity.

TASK CHAIRS

The strain on your spine from sitting with a curved spine is approximately three times greater than that from standing. To minimize this, choose a chair with a back that inclines inwards to support your lumbar area, and that moves as you stretch or lean back and forwards. Ideally, the chair back should be high and wide enough to support your back and shoulders, with arm rests to take the weight off your neck and shoulders.

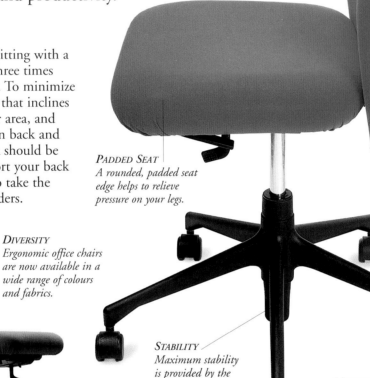

BACK SUPPORT
A chair with an adjustable back provides proper support for the user, whatever their height.

PRACTICAL FABRICS
Choose a chair with a hard-wearing wool or polyester fabric cover. A removable cover is easily cleaned or replaced to fit a new colour scheme.

◁ *TOTAL ADJUSTABILITY*
This chair has much to recommend it as a task chair: it is height-adjustable, it tilts backwards and forwards, and it has a wide supportive back, padded seat, integral lumbar support, and stable five-star base.

PADDED SEAT
A rounded, padded seat edge helps to relieve pressure on your legs.

DIVERSITY
Ergonomic office chairs are now available in a wide range of colours and fabrics.

STABILITY
Maximum stability is provided by the five-star base, which allows you to move around freely without fear of the chair tipping over.

MOBILITY
A heavy chair is easier to manoeuvre if fitted with castors.

REMEMBER

■ Make sure that your task chair complies with national regulations, especially if you employ someone at home.

■ Allow about 1m (39in) of floor space between the desk and another piece of furniture or wall, so that you can get in and out of your chair easily.

■ Think long-term and choose seating that is likely to stay in production. Otherwise, if your business develops and you have to expand your office, you may end up with odd chairs.

CHAIR ADJUSTABILITY

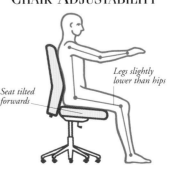

Knees form right angle

Feet flat on floor

Legs slightly lower than hips

Seat tilted forwards

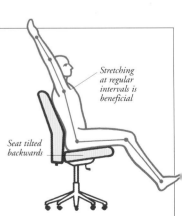

Stretching at regular intervals is beneficial

Seat tilted backwards

UPRIGHT POSITION
Place your feet flat on the floor or on a footrest, so that your legs form a right angle. Allow enough space for a fist between the seat edge and your knees.

FORWARD TILT
A chair with forward tilt allows you to reach across your desk without tipping up the chair. It also lets you occasionally sit with your legs lower than your hips.

BACKWARD TILT
With an adjustment allowing backward tilt, you can stretch tired limbs and reach objects at the side of the desk without tipping the chair over.

HEADREST
An office chair with head support is the ultimate in luxury, allowing you to lean back and relax from time to time.

ARM RESTS
Adjustable arm rests help to support your shoulders and wrists. Make sure that they are recessed so you can pull the chair close to your desk.

SPINAL SUPPORT
The chair's contours follow the natural curves of the spine, providing support to the lumbar region.

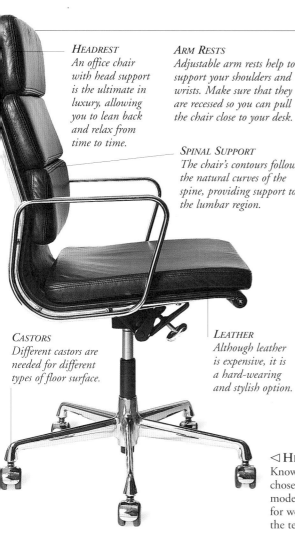

CASTORS
Different castors are needed for different types of floor surface.

LEATHER
Although leather is expensive, it is a hard-wearing and stylish option.

STATE-OF-THE-ART FABRIC △
Upholstered in a fabric that allows air circulation, good support, and even weight distribution, this chair is designed to adjust to the user's range of movements, providing proper support at all times.

◁ **HIGH-BACK CHAIR**
Known as an executive chair, and often chosen as a status symbol, this high-backed model with head support is a good option for workers who spend much of the day on the telephone or talking to people.

ACCESSORIES

For workers using an ergonomic task chair, accessories are unnecessary. However, if you use a household chair, or already suffer from back problems, adding a wedge cushion or lumbar roll can give extra comfort and help to prevent back strain.

△ **DRAFTING CHAIR**
Higher than a normal task chair, a drafting chair enables the user to work at an angled drawing board. A well-designed drafting chair is height-adjustable, with an upholstered seat for comfort, a circular foot support, and castors for mobility.

LUMBAR SUPPORT
This drafting chair has an integral lumbar support for long-term seating comfort.

FOOT BAR
A circular bar supports the feet, helping to ensure correct posture when seated.

△ **BACK SUPPORT**
A lumbar roll gives extra support to the small of the back, and helps to prevent slouching. Most attach to the chair by straps and come in removable covers for easy washing.

△ **WEDGE CUSHION**
A wedge-shaped cushion, placed on a hard seat, gives padding and comfort. Its tapered design helps to correct poor posture, in the same way as a forward-tilt mechanism.

△ **FOOTREST**
A footrest can help to relieve pressure on the thighs. It also enables you, if you are short, to keep your knees at right angles to the floor and still be at the correct height for your desk.

OCCASIONAL SEATING

ADDITIONAL SEATING, to cater for visiting colleagues and clients, meetings, and for relaxation, must be comfortable and stable. If space is at a premium, do not overlook stacking or folding chairs, which can be stored when not in use, or chairs that can be used in other parts of your home.

OFFICE-STYLE CHAIR

If you do not spend more than a couple of hours a day at your desk, a traditional office-style chair will probably be adequate. Such chairs have some ergonomic features, such as height adjustability, but will not give you full support. Avoid using kitchen or dining-room chairs for office work, as most provide no back support and will not be the correct height.

TYPIST'S CHAIR ▽
A traditional typist's chair, although height-adjustable, is adequate only for short-term use as the separate back section does not provide full support to the lumbar region.

FLEXIBILITY
The back section can be adjusted in height and moved in and out from the seat.

HARD SEAT
If used for long, a wooden seat can put pressure on your legs, leading to poor circulation.

EASY TO ADJUST
The chair height is adjusted by pressing the gas lift lever.

SOFT COVER
Personalize your ch by covering it with fabric of your choi

CASTORS
Even a fairly light chair is easier to move on castors.

ANTIQUE ALTERNATIVE △
This upholstered nineteenth-century office chair is adjustable and has a pivoting base.

WOODEN DESK CHAIR △
Natural wood is an attractive option for a modern-style office, as well as being hardwearing and easy to clean.

SPACE-SAVING SEATING

There is no shortage of options for space-saving seating; your choice will depend on your budget and the likely frequency of use. Well-designed, colourful, stacking and folding furniture doesn't take up valuable storage space when not in use; stacked up or hung on the wall, it can provide an attractive feature in the office.

STACKING STOOLS ▷
Stools are an excellent space-saving option as they can be stacked or stored under a table. However, they are not suitable for prolonged sitting as they provide no back support.

STABILITY
It is worth investing in good quality, heavy stools for improved stability.

STACKING LIMIT
Stack no more than five chairs at a time to ensure stability.

STACKING CHAIRS △
Good quality, colourful seating helps to brighten up a room. You may find a trolley useful when moving around a stack of chairs.

△ **FOLDING CHAIRS**
Though folding chairs are often a cheaper option, they are less sturdy and comfortable than stacking chairs. However, to save space they can be hung on the wall where they provide a decorative feature.

SOFT SEATING

One of the advantages of working at home is that you can tailor the surroundings to your own comfort. There is no reason why you shouldn't sit in an easy chair while you are reading, or thinking, or even taking a tea break. The easy chair can double as a welcoming reception-area chair for visitors to your home office.

TUB CHAIR ▽

Small yet comfortable seating such as the tub chair is often seen in commercial office reception areas, where its compact shape saves space. A tub chair is equally suitable in a home office, providing ideal seating for a relaxed business meeting, or in a waiting area.

STYLE AND COMFORT
A reclining chair with a separate foot rest provides a superb place to read, relax, and think.

COMPACT AND COLOURFUL
Upholstered in bright red leather, this chair brings warmth to an office environment.

△ RECLINING CHAIR

Although a comfortable chair for reading and relaxation may seem like an unnecessary luxury in the office, research shows that short breaks from work, spent resting, can enhance productivity.

CUSHIONS AND COVERS
Introduce colour, warmth, and individuality into your home office with cushions, chair covers, and throws. Some suppliers will cover chairs in a fabric supplied by the customer.

INSTANT COVER
A throw provides an instant and inexpensive colour change for chairs and sofas.

SOFA BED ▷

If you are using a spare bedroom as your home office, a sofa bed can provide soft seating for visitors during the day, and a comfortable bed for overnight guests. It can also be easily reincorporated into your home if you have to change your office back into a bedroom at some point in the future.

WORKSURFACES

CHOICE OF WORKSURFACE depends primarily on the type of work you do. The needs of a laptop user, for example, will be different from those of a worker with a large array of equipment. If you work full time, you may need a large, fitted desk, whereas a part-time worker may prefer a worksurface that can be concealed when not in use. Style is another consideration, especially if your office is part of a living area.

FITTED DESKS

If you want a permanent home office and need a large worksurface, a fitted desk is a good choice. It can be built along an entire wall, round a corner, and be adapted to fit awkward and narrow spaces. If it has to support heavy equipment, ensure that it is fitted with strong brackets and supports.

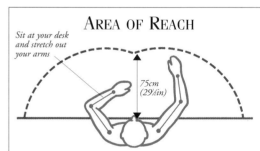

△ **ERGONOMIC CURVES**
The soft lines of a curved worktop not only create a pleasing, organic look, but also make it easier to reach every part of the desk. For a cheaper version, make your own from medium-density fibreboard (MDF).

◁ **FITTED L-SHAPED DESK**
Ideal for computer work, this desk fits neatly into the corner of a room and makes good use of natural light. There is plenty of room for the task chair to be moved around the work area, as well as integral storage for a computer hard drive and filing.

AREA OF REACH

Sit at your desk and stretch out your arms

75cm (29½in)

Make sure that frequently used equipment, such as the telephone, keyboard, and current files, are within easy reach. For most people this will be about 75cm (29½in) from their body when seated.

DESK EDGES

The choice of desk edges is important, not just because of the way they look, but also because sharp or uneven edges can cause injuries to you, your clothing, and to your equipment. Most desk manufacturers offer a choice of at least three desk-edge options – usually straight, bullnose, and waterfall.

△ **STRAIGHT**
Although still a very common option, a sharp, straight edge can cause injury and split rubber cables.

△ **BULLNOSE**
A more rounded edge, known as a bullnose, is less likely to dig into your arms, or to chip.

△ **WATERFALL**
A tapered edge, such as the waterfall, helps protect against injury, but it chips more easily than a bullnose.

FREESTANDING DESKS

Unlike the fitted desks most commonly associated with commercial offices, traditional desks, such as secretaires (with an upper cabinet) and kneehole desks, have an established place in the home. They are available in a range of styles, from hi-tech to traditional, and in a variety of materials, from glass and steel to different types of wood.

DRAWERS
Shallow drawers are useful for storing stationery and writing equipment.

ROLL-TOP COVER
Simply pull down the roll-top cover to conceal evidence of the day's work.

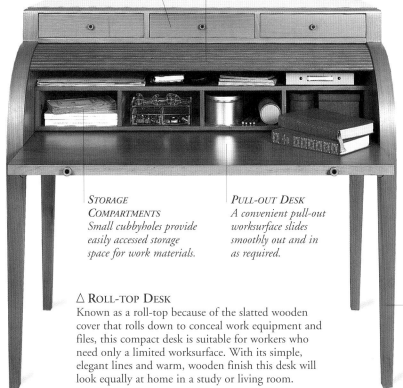

STORAGE COMPARTMENTS
Small cubbyholes provide easily accessed storage space for work materials.

PULL-OUT DESK
A convenient pull-out worksurface slides smoothly out and in as required.

△ ROLL-TOP DESK
Known as a roll-top because of the slatted wooden cover that rolls down to conceal work equipment and files, this compact desk is suitable for workers who need only a limited worksurface. With its simple, elegant lines and warm, wooden finish this desk will look equally at home in a study or living room.

△ KNEEHOLE DESK
Solid desks such as these can be expensive and difficult to move because of their weight, but generous storage space is provided by drawers in the two pedestals and under the worktop. Beware of using antique desks for heavy computer equipment.

ELEGANT LINES
The elegantly tapering legs continue the unbroken line from the curves holding the roll-top cover.

REMEMBER

■ As a guideline, standard measurements for desks are 73–75cm (28½–29½in) for height, and 140–180cm (4½–6ft) for length. A height-adjustable task chair will fit under most desks.

■ When choosing a desk, make sure that its surface is suitable for your work. If you need a hardwearing surface, select one that is heat- and stain-resistant, and that can be replaced or revarnished if necessary (*see pp.44–45*).

■ If you opt for a fitted desk, measure and list your desk-top equipment to make sure that it will all fit onto the worksurface. Drill holes in the desktop to allow power cables to feed through to sockets. Check that storage pedestals will fit underneath.

WORK TABLES

Providing the simplest and least expensive form of worksurface, a table can be used for a wide range of work from computer-based to craft activities, and will probably offer you more working surface than a desk. A kitchen or dining table is suitable, but bear in mind that heavy equipment may mark polished or softer wooden surfaces.

TRESTLE TABLE ▷
If space or your budget are limited, a trestle table provides an inexpensive worksurface that can be easily stored. However, trestle legs may be a little unsteady.

WORKSURFACE
The melamine surface is hardwearing, durable, and easily cleaned. It will not be marked by heavy equipment.

TRESTLE LEGS
Although they are easily stored when the desk is not required, trestle legs leave little room for under-desk storage.

COMPUTER DESKS

TODAY'S FURNITURE designers are acutely aware of the needs of computer users, and they have created desks that are not only practical but also look good. The desks come in a variety of styles, from the hi-tech to the traditional, with good cabling systems and spacious worksurfaces for equipment. Shop around – you'll find that computer desks can be more than just functional.

CONTEMPORARY DESKS

Instead of the traditional L-shaped desk, consisting of a worksurface and return for work equipment, contemporary desks have a more pleasing, organic shape, with soft curves substituted for sharp corners and unfriendly edges, and pastel shades and patterned laminates instead of grey melamine. Most also have cable management facilities, so work out your requirements and select a desk that is appropriate for your system.

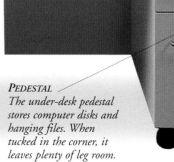

BACK VIEW
The panel hides the back of the computer, unattractive cabling, and any clutter on the floor beneath the desk.

CABLE SCREEN
Power cables run through ducting in the screen to floor sockets.

GLARE PREVENTION
A non-reflective worksurface prevents glare on the computer screen.

△ **DISCREET COMPUTER DESK**
If most of your work is computer based, a small desk may be adequate. This model will look at home in a contemporary-style room, and has a panel to conceal cables so that the rear view is uncluttered.

MOBILE SHELF
A filing tray slots into holes in the screen. Additional trays can be added if required.

DESK SURFACE
Plastic laminate offers a hardwearing, easily cleaned worksurface.

CURVED END
A rounded, extended end provides a useful small meeting area around the desk.

PARTIAL SCREEN
The half-height screening panel offers a degree of privacy, which is useful if you work in a living area.

LEGS
Power cables from the computer are channelled through the legs of the desk.

△ **ROUND-ENDED DESK**
A modern version of the L-shaped desk, or desk with return, this model is large enough for computer- and paper-based work and provides discreet cable control as well as a rounded end for meetings. The matching, mobile storage pedestal can be easily moved around to suit the user's needs.

PEDESTAL
The under-desk pedestal stores computer disks and hanging files. When tucked in the corner, it leaves plenty of leg room.

MOBILE DESK

Compact, mobile computer workstations are perfect for temporary or part-time work. When not in use, they can be wheeled into a cupboard or another room. Be sure to choose a stable model that will take all your equipment, and won't topple over when it is moved. Strong castors are vital if you intend to move the desk when it is loaded with equipment.

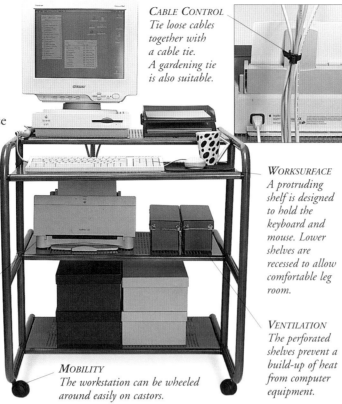

SHELVES
Deep shelves provide storage for a printer or fax machine.

THREE-TIER SYSTEM ▷
This cleverly designed, three-shelved work trolley holds a surprising amount of computer equipment and storage, but it has no worksurface for writing or paper-based work.

CABLE CONTROL
Tie loose cables together with a cable tie. A gardening tie is also suitable.

WORKSURFACE
A protruding shelf is designed to hold the keyboard and mouse. Lower shelves are recessed to allow comfortable leg room.

VENTILATION
The perforated shelves prevent a build-up of heat from computer equipment.

MOBILITY
The workstation can be wheeled around easily on castors.

CONCEALED COMPUTER DESK

If you prefer not to have your work equipment permanently on view, or if your office shares space with a living area, a concealed or disguised computer desk is the ideal option. When not in use, most of your work equipment can be stored in drawers and cupboards built into the desk. Concealing a monitor presents a problem; if you want a completely clean desk top, consider a laptop.

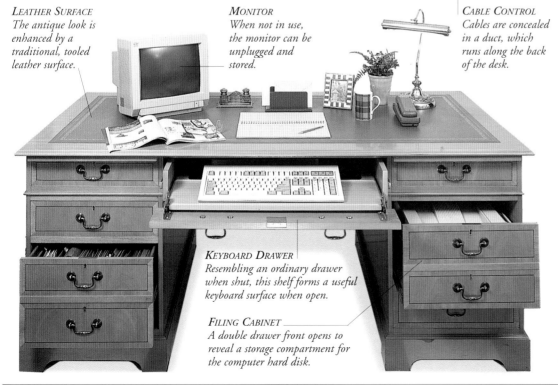

LEATHER SURFACE
The antique look is enhanced by a traditional, tooled leather surface.

MONITOR
When not in use, the monitor can be unplugged and stored.

CABLE CONTROL
Cables are concealed in a duct, which runs along the back of the desk.

KEYBOARD DRAWER
Resembling an ordinary drawer when shut, this shelf forms a useful keyboard surface when open.

FILING CABINET
A double drawer front opens to reveal a storage compartment for the computer hard disk.

COMPUTER SAFETY

Sit upright and keep your lower back supported at all times.

Tilt screen to eye level or just below, about 45cm (18in) from your face.

When working at a computer for long periods, minimize the risk of strain by holding your fingers, wrists, and lower arms in a straight line from your elbow to the keyboard.

REMEMBER

■ Establish your requirements before choosing a desk as these will affect the size of the worksurface. For example, do you need a computer with a separate hard drive, or is a laptop sufficient?

■ Do you need equipment other than a computer on your desk, such as a scanner or printer? A desk with a return or a rounded meeting end provides additional surface area for equipment.

■ Consider whether you require extra cabling facilities on your desk for your telephone and task light.

■ Some manufacturers design desks with built-in sockets hidden under a flip-up panel. These offer a neater solution than wires running across the floor to wall sockets.

◁ **ANTIQUE-STYLE DESK**
A range of desks specifically designed for computer work now offer cable management and other related facilities, disguised within a reproduction, traditional-style piece of furniture. These are available in a variety of wooden finishes from mahogany to beech.

OFFICE UNITS

SPACE EFFICIENT and increasingly popular as an alternative to the standard office set-up, office units combine a worksurface with a built-in storage facility. They are particularly useful if you have to work in the living room or bedroom and prefer to keep your work area separate from your domestic arrangements. Assess your needs first, as some units are expensive and not all are suitable for computer-based work.

MOBILE UNITS

Ranging from a complete office-on-wheels to a simple pedestal, mobile units can be closed up to conceal work equipment and moved out of the way when not in use. Smaller units are unsuitable if you have extensive computer and cabling needs, but are ideal for laptop users, workers with limited space, and part-time workers.

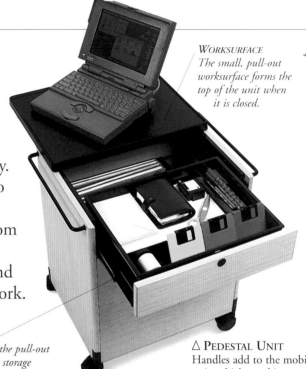

WORKSURFACE
The small, pull-out worksurface forms the top of the unit when it is closed.

CLOSED UNIT
When closed, the unit is small enough to be stored in a cupboard or pushed under a table. Light in weight, the unit has handles and castors to provide easy mobility.

STORAGE SPACE
A drawer beneath the pull-out worksurface allows storage space for accessories and files.

△ **PEDESTAL UNIT**
Handles add to the mobility of this light unit, which combines a small worksurface with storage provision consisting of a drawer and space for hanging files.

FOLD-OUT UNIT ▽
A complete home office folds out from the trunk of this cleverly designed mobile unit. It provides ample worktop space, including a pull-out shelf for a computer keyboard or laptop, a useful privacy screen, and an extended worksurface.

CLOSED UNIT
The entire office unit, with equipment stored inside, closes into a box on wheels. The worksurface legs fold up to double as handles.

REMEMBER

■ Consider your cabling requirements, as most units have limited integral cable management facilities.

■ Office units are not suitable if your work demands easy access to large quantities of files, books, other reference materials, and equipment.

■ If you are considering buying a unit, make sure that it suits your needs and that it will not become redundant if your business expands. Some units, especially mobile or disguised models, are costly.

■ Remember the storage of your task chair. If your office is concealed during out-of-work hours, choose one that matches the decor or one on castors that can be wheeled out of sight when not in use.

PINBOARD
Conveniently situated above the worksurface, a pinboard holds personal and work notices.

MARKER BOARD
A useful feature is the wipe-clean marker board and pen-rest.

SLIDING SHELF
A pull-out shelf provides space for a computer.

LOCKABLE WHEELS
The castors can be locked.

DISGUISED UNITS

The office-in-a-cupboard is a modern version of the traditional secretaire. When closed, it resembles a piece of domestic furniture, but inside, a compact yet comprehensive office is stored. A disguised unit is particularly useful in a dual-purpose space (*see pp.54–57*), allowing you to conceal files and work equipment within a unit or cupboard that suits a domestic environment, such as a kitchen.

EASY TO CONCEAL
Close the doors when you finish work for the day.

SLIDING SHELF
The keyboard remains in place when the shelf is pushed in and the cupboard closed.

CLOSED UNIT
When closed, the unit resembles a kitchen cupboard, giving no hint of the office that is contained within.

DEEP SHELVING
The large, deep shelf is suitable for storing books, files, and reference material.

TIDY DESK
Shallow drawers are useful for storing small items such as computer disks, stationery, pens, and accessories.

CUBBY HOLE
A large, deep recess provides convenient space for heavy and bulky items such as computer equipment.

◁ **OFFICE-IN-A-CUPBOARD**
This wooden cupboard is specifically designed as a complete home office, but would not look out of place in a kitchen. It is cable-managed to power points behind, making it ideal for computer-based work.

OPEN UNITS

If you are a neat, well-organized worker, an open unit can provide a simple and satisfactory home office. A variety of ready-made units are available, but you could make your own from medium-density fibreboard (MDF) – an inexpensive material that can be painted or varnished to blend with surrounding decor. Units can be wall-mounted or freestanding, but make sure that they are strong enough and securely fixed to bear the weight of work equipment.

DESIGNED FOR COMFORT
A deep worksurface allows plenty of leg room as well as space for file storage.

BOX COMPARTMENTS
Neat, box-shaped storage compartments help to keep files and books in order.

ON DISPLAY ▷
This open unit, made from medium-density fibreboard (MDF), is attached to the wall. The spacious desktop is unsupported at the front so can hold only light equipment.

Meeting Areas

Most home workers require a place to hold meetings with clients and colleagues. Give careful thought to how much room is needed and how private the space should be. Access is an issue too: you may want to avoid having clients wandering through your home to reach the meeting. A dedicated room is not always necessary as you can section off a space in your living room or office with room dividers, such as freestanding screens. If possible, locate your meeting area near to drinks facilities, an especially important point if you receive large groups of visitors.

Formal Meeting Areas

If your work requires regular meetings in which uninterrupted quiet is necessary, a formal meeting area may be the solution. Choose furniture that is comfortable, but not homely, indicating that this area is for work, not relaxation. Opt for a space where there will be no through traffic, and where you can shut the door to block out domestic noise.

PENDANT LIGHT
An overhead light that illuminates the whole table surface is ideal for a meeting area.

VENETIAN BLINDS
Blinds control the sunlight that floods in through the large window.

△ Shared Dining and Meeting Room
In many homes, the dining room offers the best meeting space but it often requires additional ambient lighting so that the room does not appear gloomy. If the meeting table is near a window, make sure you can control the natural light with blinds or curtains.

MEETING TABLE
A circular table is often the most successful option for meetings; it is considered democratic as no one sits at the head and dominates.

Informal Meeting Areas

A conventional meeting space may not be necessary if your meetings take the form of informal discussions or creative brain stormings. To create a relaxed meeting area, atmosphere and comfort are a priority, but so too is practicality. For example, although sofas and easy chairs are fine for general discussions, they are inconvenient if you need to refer to papers. Indeed, some people feel uneasy without the presence of a table to denote work. If this is the case, a quiet area in the corner of the office, or sitting round the kitchen table might be a better option. In fine weather, hold meetings in the garden or on a terrace to take advantage of the fresh air. Bear in mind likely distractions though.

ROOM DIVIDERS

Use a screen to separate your office from your meeting area or your meeting area from the living area. A screen can provide a helpful visual break that prevents the eye from being distracted by office clutter or by others working in the room. If your office is part of your living space, a screen creates a physical division between work and leisure at the end of a working day. For a more permanent separation, consider room dividers which pull out from the wall and offer better acoustic control than screens.

△ **FREESTANDING SCREENS**
Choose a screen that is stable and heavy, but not too weighty to move. You can buy semi-transluscent screens that let through light or fully opaque screens to provide a total block.

▽ **BLIND DIVIDER**
Venetian blinds make inexpensive room dividers. Good quality, heavy blinds made of wood or metal are most effective as they do not buckle or damage easily.

SOFT SEATING
The living area is ideal for hosting comfortable informal meetings. The adjacent workstation is disguised behind a blind.

ADAPTABLE BLINDS
There are several advantages to using a venetian blind as a space divider: closed it blocks out light, open it lets light in, and, when not needed, it can be drawn up.

PINE TABLE
An antique pine table strikes an informal note and provides plenty of space for paper work.

△ **KITCHEN MEETINGS**
For informal meetings, the kitchen offers a relaxed, friendly, and welcoming environment at the heart of your home, with the added advantage of access to food and drinks. If other people are at home during the day, it may not be suitable for regular long sessions, as you could find yourself at the centre of domestic activity and noise.

REMEMBER

■ Choose an area that is light and airy, conducive to inspiring thoughts and productive meetings. No-one wants to meet in a gloomy environment.

■ If your meeting space is limited, consider a fold-down table with stackable stools or chairs.

■ A meeting table can double up as a spare desk but it will need to be cleared before meetings.

WORKSTATION STORAGE

Good organization of frequently used items close to your desk is vital to working efficiently. Begin by considering which items you use regularly. Then decide whether you need to store these on your desk (the most immediate storage area), on nearby shelves, or in under-desk pedestals. If workstation storage is well planned, you should be able to grasp items easily by reaching up, across, or swivelling round in your chair.

EASY-REACH STORAGE

Store often-used files, papers, and books on shelves within reach of your desk and at mid-height, so that you don't have to stand up to grasp them. Avoid storing regularly used material in cupboards, as repeatedly opening doors wastes time. Thick shelves are best for office use, with strong supports to prevent bowing, instability, and an untidy appearance.

BOX FILE UNIT ▷
This unit holds open box files for storing a variety of items, such as loose papers and smaller files. When needed, a box file is placed on the desk and acts as a mini-storage unit.

FITTED FILES
Made-to-measure box files fit neatly into the compartments, creating a tidy appearance.

FIXED STORAGE ▷
Even if your shelves are built into the wall, aim to have a couple of adjustable shelves for flexibility. Use shelf dividers, so that when you remove a file, others do not fall over.

FIXED BUT FLEXIBLE
Here, whitewashed bricks form a strong support for the shelves.

REMEMBER

■ A shelf's strength depends on the material used, its thickness, and the length between supports. Check the load-bearing capacity of the wall before hanging shelves.

■ When planning your shelves, allow plenty of extra space to accommodate the inevitable expansion over several years.

■ Store frequently used items at waist height and above. Less used articles that are light should be kept on high shelves. Heavy items that are also used less frequently should be stored low down where they can be reached safely.

STORAGE SYSTEMS

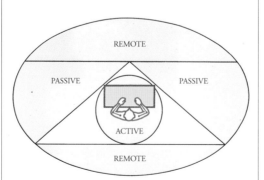

Storage areas in the work space can be divided into three zones: **active** denotes frequently used material; **passive** denotes occasionally used items; **remote** denotes rarely used articles, such as reference books. Archive storage space for old material should be kept elsewhere.

DOMESTIC STYLE
Raised up on wooden legs, this unit resembles a piece of domestic furniture.

DESKTOP STORAGE

Try to store as little as possible on your desk surface, leaving it clear for current work, your task lamp, computer, and telephone. Keep items such as pens and stationery in a desk drawer or on nearby shelves. If you have to store objects on your desk, it is neater and more efficient to keep them in containers. Use domestic objects, such as pots and mugs, as alternatives to commercial office boxes and trays.

DISK STORAGE
A drawer or box protects computer disks from dust and moisture.

BOOK ENDS
Order books on your desk in a neat row between a pair of traditional book ends.

△ **VISIBLE ACCESSORIES**
Your worksurface can quickly become unmanageable and messy if you cover it with too many loose items. Store pens, papers, and disks tidily in transparent or colourful containers.

MODULAR DESK STORAGE ▽
An upright storage system fitted to your desk allows you to clear the worksurface of everything except equipment. Wall units like this can be purchased separately or as an optional extra with shop-bought desks.

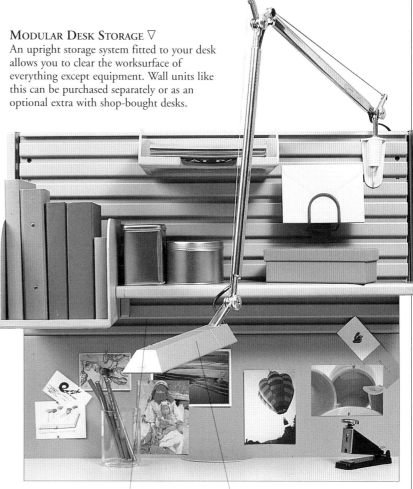

ADJUSTABLE SHELVING
Slotted into the grooves, these shelves can be moved around to suit changing needs.

SHELF-FIXED TASK LIGHT
Create more surface space by fixing your task lamp to the wall or shelf.

△ **FIXED PEDESTALS AND SHELVES**
The expansive under-desk storage space created by this double-width desk is taken up with tambour-fronted pedestals and open shelves to hold magazines and loose papers. This is a useful system if you do not have adequate wall space for shelving.

LOW/UNDER-DESK STORAGE

Floor-level storage is ideal for keeping essential items close by but out of sight. The most common form of under-desk storage is in pedestals, which can be either freestanding and mobile or built into the desk. Usually pedestals consist of a drawer and lateral space for filing, but they are also available as multiple drawer space. Unlike shelving or desk-top storage, they offer a degree of security as most pedestals are lockable.

DRAWERS ON WHEELS ▷
This trolley can be placed under or alongside a desk to provide extra drawer space. Made of durable light plastic, it can be wheeled easily between users and also serves as a central store.

CONTEMPORARY STYLE
Made from coloured plastic, this trolley offers a modern alternative to conventional office storage units.

REMOTE OFFICE STORAGE

MUCH OFFICE MATERIAL is used only occasionally but must still be accessible when required. The storage system you choose – for example fixed shelves or freestanding cabinets – and the space and position you allocate depends on the material involved. Begin by making a detailed and realistic calculation of how much remote storage space you need.

DISCREET STORAGE

Most storage systems are bulky, and it is important that they fit visually into your home. Specialized units that disguise office storage as household furniture, such as dressers, sideboards, or wardrobes, are one option. Alternatively, you can integrate conventional office storage, such as a filing cabinet, into your home by giving it a finish to match your domestic furniture.

ROLL-DOWN FLAP
Simply roll down the canvas cover to hide office equipment when not in use.

CANVAS-COVERED STORAGE ▷
Concealing shelving within a fabric cover is an inexpensive way of storing office material. Units come in a range of covers that can be coordinated to match your home.

IN DISGUISE ▷
This sideboard, which includes a drawer for hanging files, would look at home in a dining or living room. It cleverly combines open display spaces for personal items with concealed storage space for work materials.

STANDARD SHELVES
The shelves concealed behind the cupboard doors are designed to accommodate standard A4 box files and folders.

VISUAL APPEAL
The overall domestic look of this item is enhanced by the warm tones of the wood finish.

DISPLAY SPACE
Decorative objects, such as flowers and ornaments, remain displayed on the open shelves.

SIDE STORAGE
A bank of narrow, deep drawers on either side of the sideboard holds smaller items, such as pens and computer disks.

LATERAL FILING
The spacious lower drawer has been specifically designed to hold hanging files.

CLOSED UNIT
When the cupboard doors and drawers are closed, all evidence of files and other office material is concealed, leaving only decorative items on display.

OPEN SHELVES

Shelving is a cheap and flexible form of storage. Fill the full height of the room with shelving, using higher levels for rarely used materials, and the lower shelves for more frequently used items. For easy access, allow 90cm (36in) clearance in front of a row of shelves.

STRENGTH
A shelf must be thick enough to prevent sagging, and this depends on the span between supports, the material, and load. A minimum thickness of 19mm (¾in) is recommended.

STABILITY
For maximum stability, shelving supported only by brackets should not overhang the brackets by more than one sixth of the shelf width. Adjustable brackets give greater flexibility for storage.

△ NATURAL LOOK
Wooden shelving creates a softer, more homely look than metal or laminates. Fit it on a strong, wall-mounted aluminium shelving system with adjustable brackets for stability and flexibility.

◁ INDUSTRIAL STRENGTH
If your books, files, and other work materials are particularly heavy, you may require an industrial-style steel storage system, which provides shelving strong enough to hold the weightiest items.

FILING AND ARCHIVING

Don't be put off by the grey steel image of filing cabinets. Today's models come in a range of attractive colours and still provide the best system for storing files and papers. To archive materials that you no longer use but don't want to throw out, store them in steel, wood, or cardboard boxes and place them somewhere cool and dry. Keep valuable documents in a fireproof safe.

△ OVERSIZE PAPERS
A traditional plan chest holds oversize documents, such as plans, maps, and artwork. Choose a chest with an anti-curling device to keep plans flat, and check that the drawers open smoothly, even when full. An alternative is to roll up large papers and store them in a dustbin or similar container.

DUAL-PURPOSE BOX ▷
Designed for the storage of hanging files, this neat box is fitted with castors for easy mobility. When the lid is closed, the box can be used as a small occasional table.

REMEMBER

■ Place filing cabinets on an even floor surface so that the drawers glide open smoothly.

■ If you require substantial filing space, consider a lateral cabinet, which holds more material by volume than a traditional vertical unit.

■ Store files and papers in a basement only if it is dry.

■ For comfort and safety, allow 1m (3ft 3in) clearance in front of a filing cabinet.

■ Store valuable papers in acid-free boxes to prevent them from yellowing.

NATURAL LIGHT

ACCESS TO natural light is an important factor in creating a healthy and comfortable office environment. One of the advantages of working at home is that you can position your workstation to use any available light to your best advantage.

Natural light is superior to artificial light in two important ways: it is evenly distributed and therefore doesn't cast as many shadows; and, because it is less intense, it is less tiring on your eyes. However, natural light should never be relied on as the only source of light in an office, and should always be screened to prevent excessive and uncomfortable heat and glare on computer screens.

When planning your home office, consider which rooms in the house receive the most even and constant natural light, and whether your work will benefit from access to more light.

CONTROLLED EXPOSURE
Evenly diffused natural light floods in through large skylights in the high ceiling.

POINTS TO CONSIDER

■ If you work in a sunny room and need good ventilation, select a window treatment that lets air in but keeps sunlight out, such as venetian blinds or louvred shutters.

■ Blinds with an aluminium backing reflect heat back out through the window, helping to prevent uncomfortable build-up of heat.

■ Check which way your room faces. If you need protection from both low winter sun and high summer sun, venetian blinds provide an attractive and flexible option.

■ A roller blind is a cheap and effective option if you require privacy only at night, and do not need to regulate the sunlight.

■ Before opting for frosted glass, check the effect by placing tracing paper over the window.

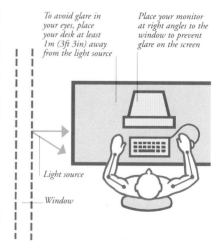

■ Even if your windows are very high, or unusually shaped, roller blinds can be made to measure and specially fitted with strings or hooks so they can be operated from below.

■ If a skylight is the only source of natural light in the room, make sure that it can be opened easily to provide ventilation.

■ A small window in a large office can make for a gloomy atmosphere. One option is to enlarge the existing window; or, if you would prefer a different aspect, consider installing a new window on another wall.

■ As long-term exposure to sunlight will eventually fade books, files, and soft furnishings, make sure that where possible you install blinds or screens to filter out the strongest rays. Try not to place such vulnerable items in direct sunlight.

WORKING WITH NATURAL LIGHT

To avoid glare in your eyes, place your desk at least 1m (3ft 3in) away from the light source

Place your monitor at right angles to the window to prevent glare on the screen

Light source

Window

If your workstation is positioned close to a sunny window, make sure that it is at right angles to the light source and a short distance away. This will help to prevent glare on your computer screen and direct sunlight in your eyes, both of which can lead to eyestrain and headaches.

ROLLER BLINDS

Simple, inexpensive roller blinds can be made from a wide range of fabrics and treated to be flame retardant.

ADVANTAGES
• Offer good protection from solar glare.
• Thick, dark blinds provide total blackout.
• Can be fitted to skylights.

DISADVANTAGES
• Can be difficult to subtly adjust light levels.
• Flap around when the window is open.
• Fabric can buckle or fade.

VENETIAN BLINDS

These blinds allow a total or partial sun block and can be adjusted to suit winter and summer sunlight.

ADVANTAGES
• Adjustable control of sunlight and privacy.
• Available in wood, aluminium, or plastic.
• Allow good air circulation.

DISADVANTAGES
• Can suggest an office environment.
• Slats are difficult to clean and attract dust.
• Cheaper versions will warp and break.

VERTICAL BLINDS

Although strongly reminiscent of commercial office decor, vertical blinds are highly effective in controlling light.

ADVANTAGES
• Made in long lengths to cover large areas.
• Allow good air circulation.
• Can be backed to control glare and heat.

DISADVANTAGES
• Not a particularly attractive option.
• Lack the flexibility of venetian blinds.
• Overtly commercial look.

CURTAINS

If your office is part of your living space, curtains are an attractive option that can warm up an otherwise cold room.

ADVANTAGES
• Help to create a more homely atmosphere.
• When closed give high level of privacy.
• Insulate against the cold.

DISADVANTAGES
• Have to be completely shut to block sunlight.
• Expensive over a large area, especially if lined.
• Inappropriate in hi-tech office.

SHUTTERS

Shutters offer an interesting alternative to curtains or blinds. Added light control is provided by those with adjustable slats.

ADVANTAGES
• Slatted models still allow ventilation when shut.
• Locked shutters add extra security.
• For privacy, use only on lower part of window.

DISADVANTAGES
• Expensive as they have to be custom-made.
• Not suitable for oddly shaped windows.
• Can cut out too much light in winter.

FROSTED GLASS

This effect is created by sandblasting the glass or by adding a special frosting film, both of which can be patterned.

ADVANTAGES
• Lets in light but provides privacy.
• Produces good diffused light.
• Relatively cheap and requires no maintenance.

DISADVANTAGES
• Gives little protection against glare and heat.
• Sandblasting of glass is permanent.
• Ineffective when window is opened.

ARTIFICIAL LIGHT

CAREFUL PLANNING is vital if the right lighting levels are to be achieved in your work area. Light that is either too strong or too weak can be counterproductive: particularly low levels impair efficiency and concentration, while excessive brightness tires your eyes, leading to eyestrain and headaches, glare on the computer screen, and unpleasant heat.

To achieve the right kind and strength of light, opt for a combination of task lighting, which throws a directed beam onto your work area, and some form of diffused ambient light. Task lighting can be provided by a clip-on, freestanding, or wall- or ceiling-mounted adjustable lamp. If your work requires natural light but there is no window nearby, consider a lamp fitted with a halogen bulb. Your choice of ambient lighting depends on personal preference and the atmosphere you wish to create in your work place.

DIFFUSED AND DIRECT LIGHT
A desk lamp, overhead light, and spotlight combine to produce effective office lighting.

POINTS TO CONSIDER

■ Place your task light on the opposite side to your writing hand to prevent shadows falling on your work as you write.

■ If reducing energy consumption is an important priority for you, choose lamps and light fittings that can be fitted with long-life, compact fluorescent bulbs.

■ If you regularly suffer from eyestrain and headaches while working, the level of light in your work area may be insufficient. Remember that older workers require a considerably higher light level than younger workers. Adjust the level until it is comfortable for you.

■ Inadequate lighting in the work place can lead to bad posture, such as sitting hunched up in front of a computer screen in order to be able to see it better. This, in turn, may result in neck, shoulder, and back strain.

■ When choosing lamps and fittings, be aware of the kind of light generated from the different bulbs. Traditional tungsten lighting produces a warm colour cast, but generates a lot of heat and the bulbs require frequent replacement. Many modern light fixtures are fitted with compact fluorescent tubes, which are miniaturized versions of the lighting commonly used in offices. These consume 20 per cent less energy and throw out less heat than tungsten bulbs, but the light is cool and somewhat harsh. Halogen bulbs provide the most natural colour balance, and have the advantage of supplying a great deal of light from a relatively small source.

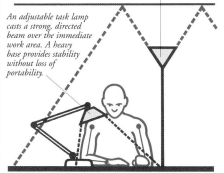

■ A freestanding, combined up- and downlighter, which provides a flexible and easily portable source of good general diffused light, is an option if you do not want to go to the expense and inconvenience of altering your electrical wiring to install ceiling- or wall-mounted lights.

OPTIMUM LIGHTING

An uplighter bounces rays off the ceiling, producing a diffused light with no strong shadows.

An adjustable task lamp casts a strong, directed beam over the immediate work area. A heavy base provides stability without loss of portability.

Combine lamps that provide generalized, indirect illumination with adjustable desk-top lighting. Light should be strongest in your work area, but weaker and diffused elsewhere. Try to achieve a gradation in light contrast levels from the desk to the background as this is easier on your eyes than an abrupt change or none at all.

TASK LIGHTING

DESK LIGHT

A desk lamp with a flexible arm gives a strong, directed, easily adjusted light onto the immediate work area.

ADVANTAGES
• Throws light onto a specific area.
• Can be easily moved about.
• No direct glare from light source.

DISADVANTAGES
• Takes up valuable desk-top space.
• Generates heat and can be hot to touch.
• Unstable if base is not heavy enough.

CLIP-ON SPOTLIGHT

Simple to attach to shelves and walls, and easily moveable, a clip-on spot provides a strong, directed beam.

ADVANTAGES
• Can be moved around as required.
• Takes up no desk-top space.
• Cannot be knocked over.

DISADVANTAGES
• Lacks the flexibility of a desk light.
• Must be unclipped to change light direction.
• Trailing flex can be unsightly.

DOWNLIGHTER

Providing medium light distribution with a directional beam, this is also available as a ceiling-mounted model.

ADVANTAGES
• Floor-standing models are portable.
• Avoids flex trailing over the desk.
• Wide variety of styles available.

DISADVANTAGES
• Can take up valuable floor space.
• More expensive than desk-top lights.
• May be easily knocked over.

AMBIENT LIGHTING

UPLIGHTER

Providing evenly diffused light without glare, uplighters are available as wall-mounted and floor-standing models.

ADVANTAGES
• Gives evenly diffused background light.
• Provides an attractive room feature.
• Floor-standing models are portable.

DISADVANTAGES
• Wall-mounted models cannot be moved.
• Floor-standing models take up floor space.
• Not suitable in a room with a dark ceiling.

ADJUSTABLE SPOTLIGHT

A wall- or ceiling-mounted spotlight, offering 360° rotation and 180° pivot, provides flexible background lighting.

ADVANTAGES
• Distributes light evenly.
• Independent or central switch.
• Takes up to 100 watt reflector bulb.

DISADVANTAGES
• Permanent fixture, so cannot be moved.
• May require new wiring by electrician.
• Light is focused rather than diffused.

TABLE LAMP

Providing soft diffused lighting with a more homely feel, a traditional table lamp can soften the office atmosphere.

ADVANTAGES
• Can be easily moved around.
• Less expensive than floor lamps.
• No glare, as the bulb is not exposed.

DISADVANTAGES
• Smaller and less robust than office lights.
• Area illuminated may be quite small.
• May appear too cosy for work place.

OFFICE TECHNOLOGY

SOPHISTICATED TECHNOLOGY has opened the way to successful home working in many previously office-based occupations, enabling workers to produce professional-quality work at home and to communicate easily with colleagues and clients. But technology is constantly changing – it has been predicted that by the year 2010, desktop computers will be up to a million times more powerful than they are today – so, when working out your requirements, seek the advice of specialists who will help you to decide on the best options for your particular type of work.

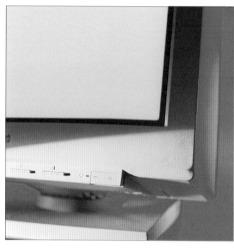

VDU

If you use a visual display unit (VDU), be sure to adopt good working practices in order to avoid health problems.

POINTS TO CONSIDER
• Choose a VDU that can tilt and swivel, so that you can angle it correctly for your eye level.
• Invest in quality – inferior quality screens can cause eye strain.
• If you are unable to eliminate glare on your screen, cover it with a screen shade.
• Buy a screen saver program to safeguard the screen when you leave it unattended.

HI-TECH OFFICE
An ultra-modern office, which makes a clear statement about the owner's personality and interests.

FAX

Sending copies of documents by fax, via the telephone network, is now the most common form of communication.

POINTS TO CONSIDER
• If you are linked to the Internet or a modem, you may not require a separate fax machine.
• Fax machines can be noisy, so they are best situated away from your workstation.
• If you use both telephone and fax machine frequently, a combined model, sharing one telephone line, may not be sufficient. Consider installing a dedicated fax line.

POINTS TO CONSIDER

■ If you work at home for a company, look into linking to their computer system via a modem, which enables computer files to be transmitted over the telephone network. It can give you access to the Internet, allowing you to send letters and faxes to other users electronically – saving time, paper, and postage costs.

■ A fax machine can be used to copy documents, and may eliminate the need for an expensive photocopier.

■ Video or audio conferencing is an option for people who find it inconvenient or difficult to travel to meetings away from home.

■ Noisy equipment can become a source of irritation, so check on this when making your choice. A maximum of 55 decibels (the level of normal conversation) is ideal.

■ If mobility is important, invest in a laptop with integral modem rather than desktop models. Opt for a mobile phone that will accept calls diverted from the office.

■ As home workers do not have the luxury of a computer support team to assist with problems, investigate computer service agreements and help lines.

■ Make sure that you conform to health and safety regulations.

PRINTER

Buy the best printer you can afford: it will save you time and help to project a professional image in your work.

POINTS TO CONSIDER
• Choose a printer that is as quiet as possible. If your printer is noisy, a printer hood may keep disturbance to a minimum.
• Placing a foam mat under the printer will help to reduce noise and vibration.
• Your choice of printer will depend on the type of work you do and your budget, so discuss your requirements with specialists.

KEYBOARD

Keyboards vary in size and design, but it is vital that you choose one that you can work on comfortably, without strain.

POINTS TO CONSIDER
• If possible, hire a keyboard to test out at home before buying.
• Angle the keyboard to suit your individual needs. Incorrect positioning can cause repetitive strain injury and tire back and neck muscles.
• Padded wrist rests, used in conjunction with an adjustable keyboard, can protect against strained muscles and tendons.

CABLING TIPS

Good cable management ensures that cables are distributed unobtrusively around the office. In commercial offices, cables are usually trunked through the floor, but this is rarely possible at home. Integral desk management (*see pp.28–29*) and the simple systems below can help.

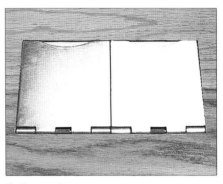

△ FLOOR SOCKETS
To avoid cables trailing across the room into wall sockets, install sockets in the floor directly below your desk. A metal casing protects the sockets from dust and damage.

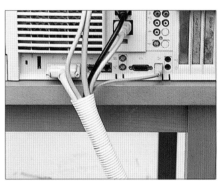

△ CABLE ORGANIZER
A neat way to organize the profusion of cables at the back of a workstation is to encase them in a specially designed plastic tube, split down its length for easy installation.

PHOTOCOPIER

Although expensive, a photocopier is worth the investment if you regularly have to make a lot of copies.

POINTS TO CONSIDER
• Weigh up the time wasted making trips to the photocopier shop against the cost of buying your own machine. If you decide to buy, invest at the same time in maintenance and repair contracts.
• Photocopiers take up space, produce heat and noise, and require good ventilation.
• If you need a photocopier but your space is limited, smaller, desktop models are available.

TELEPHONE

Telephone companies are providing an ever-expanding range of services. Call them to discuss your requirements.

POINTS TO CONSIDER
• Install a separate business line so that friends and family do not interrupt your work.
• If you have only one line, a voice mail service enables callers to leave messages when you are already on the telephone.
• Message services, run by telephone companies, remove the need for a separate answering machine and can be accessed from any phone.

△ DESK HOOKS
If your desk doesn't have cable management facilities, run cables through plastic-coated cup hooks, fitted into the back of the desk or adjacent wall, to keep them neat and safe.

SURFACES AND FINISHES

AS THE MOST PERMANENT and visible elements in your office, finishes for floors, walls, desks, and shelving require particularly careful selection. The materials, colours, and textures chosen will determine whether your work space looks warm or cool, formal or informal, and homely or businesslike. Practical considerations must also be taken into account: the cost, durability, and suitability of materials are all vital to a successful choice. Experiment with sample tiles and swatches before making a decision.

CONTRAST WITHOUT CONFLICT
The warm wood flooring and panelling contrast with the cool glass and chrome table.

POINTS TO CONSIDER

■ Not all materials are equally durable. Hardwearing, long-lasting materials may cost more initially, but they can save you money in the long run.

■ Some materials and finishes are more environmentally friendly than others, so check with the manufacturer if this is of concern to you. If you decide to use a hardwood, check that it comes from a renewable source.

■ Linoleum, although costly, is a good option for a floor covering. It is environmentally friendly, recyclable, hygienic, durable, and easy to clean and maintain.

■ Tiles and wood strip flooring must be laid on an even surface so, if this is your choice, you may have to cover the floor first with hardboard or screed.

■ Carpets and other soft furnishings help to muffle noise.

■ Medium-density fibreboard (MDF) provides an inexpensive option for a worksurface. Cut to size and varnished or painted, it makes a hardwearing, tailor-made surface.

■ Improve the appearance of a concrete floor by painting it with special hardwearing paints.

WORKSURFACES

WOOD

A natural, sustainable material that offers a range of tones from pale beech to dark mahogany or stained finishes.

ADVANTAGES
• Warm looking and warm to the touch.
• Durable. Marks and scratches can be removed.
• Adds a homely feel to an office.

DISADVANTAGES
• Some woods, such as oak, are expensive.
• Softer woods, such as beech, are liable to mark.
• Heat can damage the surface.

FLOORING

CARPET

Carpets provide comfort underfoot, and are available in tile or roll form. Special antistatic carpet is available for offices.

ADVANTAGES
• Provides sound insulation and draughtproofing.
• Cables can be safely concealed underneath.
• Extensive choice of colours and patterns.

DISADVANTAGES
• Some carpets can cause static electricity.
• Harbours dust and carpet mites.
• Thick domestic carpet will show castor marks.

PLASTIC LAMINATE

Commonly used for office desks and shelving, laminates are available in a range of qualities and finishes.

ADVANTAGES
• Wide range of colours and designs.
• Hygienic and easy to clean.
• Cheaper than solid wood.

DISADVANTAGES
• Lacks the warmth and naturalness of wood.
• Surface of cheap products may chip or peel off.
• Difficult to repair once damaged.

METAL

Stainless steel or zinc are the most common choices for metal surfaces, well suited to a hi-tech-style office.

ADVANTAGES
• Creates a strong, distinctive modern look.
• Easily cleaned with a damp cloth.
• Durable. Can be sandblasted and resealed.

DISADVANTAGES
• Reflective surface can cause glare on screen.
• Can absorb heat from equipment.
• Easily scratched by other metal items.

LEATHER AND BAIZE

Once commonly used on writing desks, leather and baize inserts can be updated in modern, vibrant colours.

ADVANTAGES
• Creates a feeling of traditional luxury.
• Can be easily replaced if damaged.
• May be used to define certain areas on desk.

DISADVANTAGES
• Stains easily and is difficult to clean.
• Can wear and tear at the edges.
• Heavy equipment will scratch and mark it.

WOOD

An attractive and hardwearing material, wood is available as stripped or painted boards, parquet, or block flooring.

ADVANTAGES
• Gives a warm, homely feeling.
• Easy to clean and maintain.
• Can be painted, stripped, or covered with rugs.

DISADVANTAGES
• Varnished surfaces need regular maintenance.
• Does not provide acoustic insulation.
• Pale woods show marks and dirt easily.

VINYL

Easy to cut to shape, vinyl is available in sheet or tile form as well as in a wide range of colours and patterns.

ADVANTAGES
• Good value for money.
• Durable and easy to maintain.
• Textured finishes and padded surfaces available.

DISADVANTAGES
• Not suitable for uneven floors.
• Can be marked by heavy furniture.
• Wood and ceramic effects are rarely convincing.

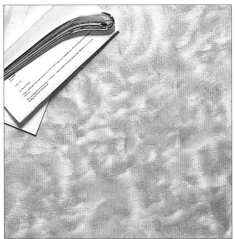

TILES

Available in ceramic, slate, marble, vinyl, or terracotta, tiles are popular as attractive, low-maintenance surfaces.

ADVANTAGES
• Easy to clean and maintain.
• Useful on floors that tend to be damp.
• Hardwearing and stain resistant.

DISADVANTAGES
• May necessitate special castors on chairs.
• Heavy metal cabinets may crack ceramic tiles.
• Tiles can feel cold underfoot.

PERSONALIZING YOUR SPACE

AN IMPORTANT ADVANTAGE of working at home is having total control over the design of your work environment, free from corporate restrictions on furniture and accessories. Personalizing your space means introducing elements that are not essential to your office, but help to define it as uniquely yours and reflect your tastes, idiosyncrasies, and requirements. From colour schemes and soft furnishings, through to pictures and plants, think about features that will aid your work by helping to create a more congenial environment, rather than acting as distractions.

THE PERSONAL TOUCH
A wall of art helps to create a highly personal environment without taking up valuable work space.

DRINKS FACILITIES

If your work area is situated far from the kitchen, create a catering area for preparing refreshments in your office.

ADVANTAGES
• Constant supply of drinks and snacks.
• Entertaining clients is made easier.
• Prevents tea breaks wasting work time.

DISADVANTAGES
• Creates mess and takes up space.
• Considerable expense of additional fridge.
• Hum of fridge may be irritating.

SOFT FURNISHINGS

Add an occasional soft furnishing, such as a lampshade or cushion to soften an otherwise impersonal work space.

ADVANTAGES
• Gives warmth and colour to an office.
• Creates a more homely atmosphere.
• Can be coordinated to tie office decor together.

DISADVANTAGES
• May not create the right image for clients.
• Will not be as durable as hard finishes.
• Not as easy to keep clean as hard finishes.

POINTS TO CONSIDER

■ Take into account how a personalized office environment might affect your attitude to work: you may be someone who requires an impersonal, businesslike environment to perform well. For example, if you find it difficult to concentrate or suffer from a lack of self discipline, visual or aural accessories, such as a television, radio, or computer games, could prove to be endlessly distracting.

■ A few executive toys or games may provide welcome interludes in your working day if you spend long periods alone in your home office. However, avoid cheap gadgets that can break and may become a source of irritation rather than stimulation and relaxation.

■ Colour profoundly affects the way you feel. The final choice is, of course, up to you, but bear in mind that cool colours, such as pale blue and green and other pastels, have a calming effect, whereas warm reds and oranges are vibrant, stimulating, and may tire your eyes. Dark colours can create a gloomy atmosphere, especially at night, but they can play a useful role in disguising a room's proportions, such as making a high ceiling seem lower.

■ If your work involves meetings with clients, consider how much of your domestic life you wish to reveal to them. Do you want them to see your domestic arrangements or would you prefer to keep work and home separate?

HOUSEHOLD PETS

If you own a pet, you need to decide whether to allow it to encroach on your office area and your professional life.

ADVANTAGES
• Provides company when working alone.
• Playing with an animal helps to relieve stress.
• Fish provide low-maintenance visual interest.

DISADVANTAGES
• Animals can be destructive.
• Distracting if they demand constant attention.
• Can leave hairs or dirt around the office.

PICTURES

More than any other item, photographs, prints, and paintings help to personalize a home office environment.

ADVANTAGES
• Communicates your personality to visitors.
• Psychologically comforting.
• Inspirational and add colour.

DISADVANTAGES
• Can be distracting.
• Take up desktop and shelf space.
• Pictures behind glass may cause glare.

PERSONALIZED TOOLS

Office tools, such as mouse mats, need not be boring; they now come in a range of designs and colours.

ADVANTAGES
• Introduces a fun element into the environment.
• Expresses your personality to visitors.
• Indicates that yours isn't a commercial office.

DISADVANTAGES
• Often more expensive than conventional items.
• Some personalized equipment is impractical.
• May be of lower quality than traditional tools.

EXECUTIVE TOYS

A variety of executive toys, designed to relieve mental and physical stress at work, are now available.

ADVANTAGES
• Squeezy toys help to relieve stiff fingers.
• Visually appealing objects help to relax eyes.
• Provide a break from work routine.

DISADVANTAGES
• Can be distracting.
• Expensive and can quickly lose novelty value.
• Take up desktop and shelf space.

PLANTS AND FLOWERS

Adding plants and flowers to your office is a relatively inexpensive way of transforming its look and atmosphere.

ADVANTAGES
• Provides instant colour and scent.
• Helps to keep you in touch with nature.
• Large plants can act as screens or space dividers.

DISADVANTAGES
• Vases can topple over and spill water.
• Plants drop leaves and pots can leak.
• Plants are unsuitable in rooms lacking daylight.

MUSIC AND RADIO

If you work alone, you may enjoy the sound of some background music or a radio programme.

ADVANTAGES
• Radios provide contact with the outside world.
• Background music can relieve stress.
• Silence can be unsettling for those used to noise.

DISADVANTAGES
• Can interfere with concentration.
• Not suitable if you use the phone frequently.
• May distract co-workers or others in the home.

DEDICATED OFFICE PLAN

A ROOM DEVOTED solely to home working has many advantages. Whether a luxurious spacious attic or a small spare room, a dedicated room gives you total privacy and the freedom to organize your space to match your working needs. This option is most suitable for people who work full time from home, who employ other workers, or who plan on expansion.

◁ ❷ SPACE FILLERS
Spaces in and around the chimney flues have been converted into deep shelves to hold large books and files. The larger bottom shelf houses storage boxes.

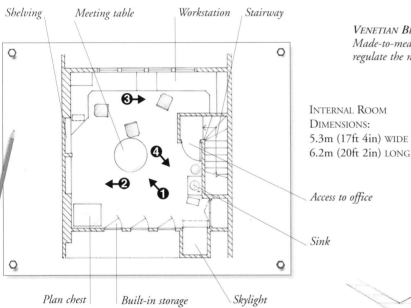

Shelving   Meeting table   Workstation   Stairway

VENETIAN BLINDS
Made-to-measure blinds regulate the natural light.

INTERNAL ROOM DIMENSIONS:
5.3m (17ft 4in) WIDE
6.2m (20ft 2in) LONG

Access to office

Sink

Plan chest   Built-in storage   Skylight

△ BIRD'S EYE VIEW
A large, square room, such as this, is one of the easiest to plan as it has no awkward spaces. Desks adjoin the wall of windows to take full advantage of the light.

CORNER DESK
A wall-fixed corner desk allows the computer monitor to be positioned at a right angle to the window to avoid glare.

FLOORING
Maple strip floor lightens the room and gives a contemporary look.

◁ ❶ CENTRAL TABLE
A round table breaks up the otherwise empty central area. It can be used for meetings and as an additional worksurface. Its proximity to shelving holding reference material makes it an ideal place for reading and research.

FOR MORE DETAILS...

Fitted shelving SEE P. 37

Fitted desks SEE P. 26

Round tables SEE PP. 32–33

Venetian blinds SEE P. 39

❸ BUILT-IN DESK AND SHELVING ▷

The white laminated fitted desk is an integral part of the fitted shelf unit, giving overall continuity of style and line. Shelves, designed to fit under the eaves, are tailor-made to hold specific pieces of equipment.

PORTHOLES
Unusual circular windows were specifically installed to shed light on a previously dark staircase.

WATER SUPPLY
The sink is situated well away from the work area and computer equipment in case of spillages.

CATERING TROLLEY
A neat trolley stores mugs, crockery, and other utensils useful for making drinks and snacks.

DESIGN POINTS

■ The first step when planning a dedicated office is to work out your power and cabling requirements. Most people considerably underestimate, so calculate how many power points you think you will need, then add a third more.

■ If the office is large, do not attempt to fill up all the space by spreading out your work and storage areas. Estimate your requirements and place the elements according to convenience and accessibility.

■ Decide whether you need a dedicated office water supply. This will depend on ease of access to the kitchen.

SKYLIGHT
An additional window lights up a gloomy area and provides ventilation.

REMOTE STORAGE
Cupboards built into the lowest part of the eaves provide storage for archive material.

PLAN CHEST
Ideal for storing oversize papers, this plan chest doubles as a worksurface.

❹ CATERING POINT ▷

A sink has been installed so that tea and coffee can be prepared in the office. A rack holds kitchen equipment, and a covered bin limits food or drink odours.

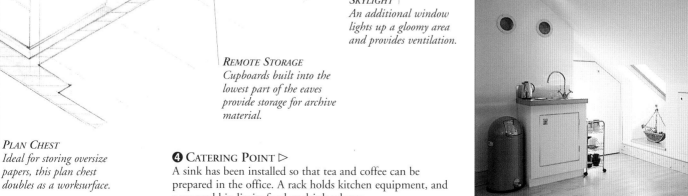

DEDICATED OFFICE CHOICE

△ ORDERED ACTIVITY
An open-plan office gives a feeling of space and light. In this room, clutter is restricted to the rear wall, forming an impression of hectic activity, but leaving space elsewhere. A drawing board is positioned to take advantage of the natural light, which is reflected throughout by the white walls.

△ FUNCTIONAL
Keep your office simple if your work activities are limited. Here, only a large worksurface is needed for laying out materials; specialist, built-in shelving holds portfolios, and a trolley provides mobile storage.

REFLECTED SPACE ▷
Reacting against the charmlessness of many commercial offices, the owner of this traditional-style mirrored study has created a more personal space, displaying family photographs and art, and filling shelves with ornaments alongside reference books.

◁ WORK AND PLAY
Bright primary colours give this home office an informal, domestic look, suggestive of both work and play. Generous built-in storage space allows files and office accessories to be completely concealed.

DUAL-PURPOSE OFFICE PLAN

IF YOU DO NOT HAVE a whole room to spare for your home office, consider a dual-purpose space, such as this office/dining room, which functions as an office in the daytime but by careful design becomes a dining room in the evening. This option requires careful planning and cleverly adaptable furniture. Firstly, decide the primary function of the room and then design the space around this decision.

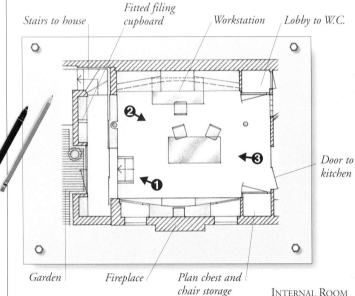

Stairs to house *Fitted filing cupboard* *Workstation* *Lobby to W.C.*

Garden *Fireplace* *Plan chest and chair storage* *Door to kitchen*

△ **BIRD'S EYE VIEW**
The desks and storage areas are placed around the perimeter, leaving a central space for meetings or a dining area.

INTERNAL ROOM DIMENSIONS:
5m (16ft) WIDE
6m (19ft 6in) LONG

STORAGE CUPBOARD
Filing can be exposed or hidden behind attractive tambour-fronted units.

FRENCH WINDOWS
Providing alternative access to the office, the French windows also flood the basement with light.

MOVEABLE STEPS
Leading to the raised level and garden, these steps can be removed at night when the sliding glass doors are closed.

FIREPLACE
A relaxed working and cosy home atmosphere is created by the fireplace.

DESIGN POINTS

■ Choose furniture that is suitable for work but does not look out of place in the home. Take advantage of multi-functional furniture.

■ Design the room around its primary function. For example, as this room is firstly an office and only used occasionally as a dining room, crockery and other items are not stored here, but in the adjacent kitchen.

■ Hide all cabling and power points behind panelling.

■ Design the storage space so that it can be easily concealed behind cupboard doors.

◁ ❶ **OUTSIDE ACCESS**
The mezzanine provides access to the garden, a separate office entrance, and further filing space. It allows as much natural light and ventilation as possible into the basement.

GLASS DOORS
Sliding glass screens help to divide the space from the stairs and doors, and reduce draughts in winter.

LOW-LEVEL STORAGE
Lateral hanging files are stored at low level for easy access.

DUAL-PURPOSE DESK
A glass table doubles as a desk and as a dining table.

OFFICE EQUIPMENT
A roll-top wooden cupboard opens to hold a computer and printer.

FOR MORE DETAILS...

Roll-top desk SEE P. 27

Plan chest SEE P. 37

Desk surfaces SEE PP. 44–45

Occasional seating SEE PP. 24–25

△ ❷ MEETING AREA
Most of the office equipment is ranged along one wall, which is the focus of the office. An extra table in the centre can be used as a second desk or as a meeting table.

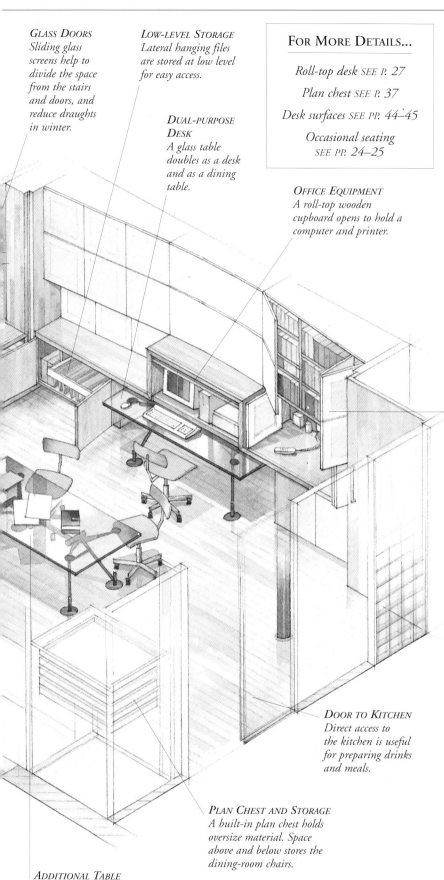

PERFORATED CUPBOARDS
The door folds back to reveal office equipment. When closed, the perforations ensure electrical equipment does not overheat.

DOOR TO KITCHEN
Direct access to the kitchen is useful for preparing drinks and meals.

PLAN CHEST AND STORAGE
A built-in plan chest holds oversize material. Space above and below stores the dining-room chairs.

ADDITIONAL TABLE
A second table can be moved around to be used as a desk, or as a meeting or dining table.

△ ❸ DINING ROOM
When work is over all evidence of the office can be closed away behind cupboard doors. The two glass-topped tables are pushed together to form a large dining table. Dining-room chairs replace the task chairs.

DUAL-PURPOSE OFFICE CHOICE

△ **UNDER-BED OFFICE**
Many manufacturers produce
raised-bed kits with a study area
below, offering a worksurface and
storage space. Although these don't
allow for expansion, they provide a
simple part-time office solution.

△ **DEFINED WORK AREA**
Guest bedrooms often double as
home offices. Denote the boundary
between work and sleep with a
raised platform, below which useful
storage space is created. A sofa, used
as additional office seating, becomes
a bed when guests come to stay.

△ **DESK/DRESSING TABLE**
A simple office space for occasional
use has been created in an alcove in
this spare bedroom, with a work
surface doubling as a dressing table.
Pastel colours and soft furnishings
help to retain a bedroom ambience.

△ **STORE-AWAY BED**
The office is permanent and the
bedroom occasional in this dual-
purpose room. A desk, fitted with
castors, can be pushed back to the
window to make room for the bed,
which is stored in a cupboard.

AMPLE STORAGE ▷
In this spacious bedroom, the
attractive drapes screen off the
substantial office storage space,
while the light, mobile workstation
can be wheeled away and stored
when work is finished.

INTEGRATED OFFICE PLAN

THE CHALLENGE OF CREATING an office in a living area is to find a way of combining the two functions without compromising privacy, or creating two small, disparate sections. Although an office that shares space with a living area is more suited to part-time work, careful and imaginative planning can produce an office suitable for full-time use. One solution is to separate work and domestic areas with a flexible partition.

DOMESTIC FOCUS
A working fireplace provides a focus for the living area.

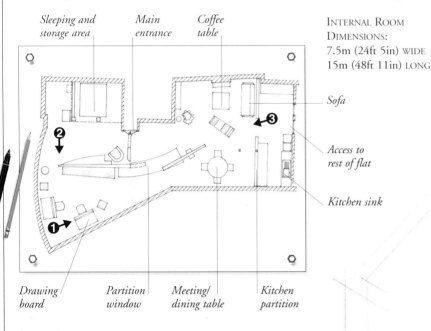

Sleeping and storage area   *Main entrance*   *Coffee table*

INTERNAL ROOM
DIMENSIONS:
7.5m (24ft 5in) WIDE
15m (48ft 11in) LONG

Sofa

❸

❷

Access to rest of flat

❶

Kitchen sink

Drawing board   *Partition window*   *Meeting/ dining table*   *Kitchen partition*

△ BIRD'S EYE VIEW
Distinct areas have been created for sleeping, living, and working in this irregularly shaped room. A freestanding, curved, central partition demarcates the office area.

SEPARATE ENTRANCE
The partition doorway allows direct access to the office, without having to walk through the living area.

△ ❶ OPEN PLAN
The office is situated in one corner of the room, but has views through to the dining area, which doubles as a meeting area, and to the living area, which is situated in the opposite corner.

HIDDEN STORE
A discreet storage space has been created above the sleeping area by building a false ceiling.

BEDROOM PRIVACY
Venetian blinds screen the sleeping area from clients and co-workers.

IMPROVISED PLAN CHEST
A galvanized steel dustbin provides convenient storage for architectural plans.

CONTINUOUS FLOORING
Wooden flooring runs throughout, integrating the separate areas.

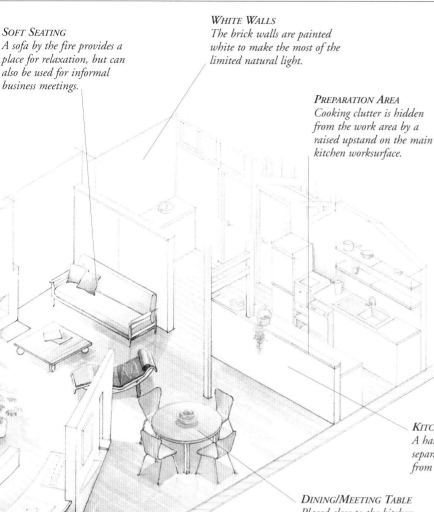

SOFT SEATING
A sofa by the fire provides a place for relaxation, but can also be used for informal business meetings.

WHITE WALLS
The brick walls are painted white to make the most of the limited natural light.

PREPARATION AREA
Cooking clutter is hidden from the work area by a raised upstand on the main kitchen worksurface.

KITCHEN PARTITION
A half-height wall separates the kitchen from the dining area.

DINING/MEETING TABLE
Placed close to the kitchen, a round dining table doubles as a meeting table.

MOBILE STORAGE
Files and work tools are stored in multi-purpose mobile units.

TASK LIGHTING
Adjustable task lights are clipped to the drawing boards, leaving adjacent floor space free.

△ **❷ PARTIAL SEPARATION**
The main work area is situated directly beneath the skylight, the room's main source of natural light. The partition is designed to allow this light to filter through to the other parts of the room.

FOR MORE DETAILS...

Drafting stool SEE P. 23

Screens SEE P. 33

Circular tables SEE P. 32

Light control SEE PP. 36–37

Mobile storage units SEE P. 35

DESIGN POINTS

■ If possible, create a separate entrance to the work area so that clients can enter the office without having to go through the living area first.

■ Store filing and equipment in cupboards rather than on shelves as this helps to leave the work area looking tidier at the end of the day.

■ Install dimmer switches for lights as it is usually preferable to have lower light levels in the evening than for work.

■ Instead of installing a fixed partition between your work and living space, consider the flexibility of venetian blinds or freestanding screens.

△ **❸ DISPLAY AND PRESENTATION AREA**
The large window in the partition has a deep windowsill that acts as a surface for displaying work or household artefacts. The partition itself also provides a presentation area for work designs on the office side, and for a personal choice of pictures and prints on the other.

Integrated Office choice

△ Discreet Office

When working and living in the same room, one design option is to keep the office discreet. This work area fits neatly between the shelving and has a mobile filing cabinet and stool that can be pushed under the desk when not in use.

Limited Space ▷

In a small, dual-purpose room, a tidy desk and generous storage space are essential. Here, the desk with pedestals, and the large storage unit keep the area uncluttered. Domestic and work furniture is co-ordinated in colour and materials.

△ Office and Home in Harmony

In a home office that is a visible and permanent part of a living space, choose office furniture and accessories that blend in with the decor of the room. Here, the chrome task chair and task light echo the chrome of the living-room chair, candlestick, and clock.

△ Room Divider

Venetian blinds make good space dividers and are especially useful when creating an office within a living area. If there is only one natural light source, they allow light to filter into both areas.

△ Space-saving Desk

The corner of a living room is often a good site for an office. Here, the task chair can be neatly pulled into the curve of the desk, which provides a spacious worksurface without imposing on the rest of the room.

CONVERSION PLAN

Converting a room such as a loft or garage, or utilizing an extension provides a blank canvas on which to create your ideal home office, and often offers the opportunity to incorporate character and unusual features into the room. Before embarking on major conversion work, consult an architect or builder and work out a plan in full.

Hallway to house *Fitted shelves line the wall* *Printer and stationery store* *Fitted desk behind window*

Photocopier and fax *Window in front of wall-length fitted desk*

△ BIRD'S EYE VIEW
By placing the extensive fitted desks and shelves against opposite walls, and leaving the central area empty, this narrow extension has enough room for up to three home workers.

INTERNAL ROOM
DIMENSIONS:
2.2m (7ft 2½in) WIDE
9.3m (30ft 3½in) LONG

FITTED TABLE
A small fitted table creates an extra surface for sorting papers and occasional work.

REMOTE STORAGE
Infrequently required inactive storage is housed in the service area, away from the workstation.

SERVICE AREA
The lobby provides a separate service area for the main office.

PARTITION WINDOW
Natural light floods into the service area through a window in the partition.

PEDESTALS
The fitted worksurface is supported by pedestals which store regularly used filing.

SECURE FILING
Metal filing cabinets provide a secure place for precious files.

DOMESTIC TOUCH
A fitted carpet helps this room maintain a warm, domestic atmosphere.

DESIGN POINTS

■ Start by assessing the room's structure and essential requirements, such as thermal insulation or damp-proofing.

■ If you require additional windows, invest in quality ones with security locks. Make sure they are draught-proofed.

■ Position all plugs and power points away from windows to prevent water seeping in and damaging them.

■ An outhouse may require extra security. If it is situated some way from the house and is accessible from the street, consider investing in a burglar alarm or secure locks.

△ ❶ USING NATURAL LIGHT
Despite its narrow shape, this light-filled room looks surprisingly spacious. This impression is achieved by a combination of the extensive windows and the bright yellow walls and white ceiling, which help to reflect the ample natural light.

❷ FROM THE OUTSIDE ▷
As a security measure, there is no door leading
directly from the garden to the office. The entrance
is either through the house, or through the service
area, which has a lockable door into the main office.

WALL OF SHELVES
*Tailor-made shelves,
fitted to cover a whole
wall, hold all the office
equipment and files.*

AMBIENT/TASK LIGHT
*This anglepoise provides
background light and
doubles as a task light for
the printer station.*

**PRINTER AND
STATIONERY**
*Storage for the
printer and stationery
are conveniently
placed together within
easy reach of the
workstation.*

REMOTE STORAGE
*Rarely used loose papers are
stored high up in box and
ring files.*

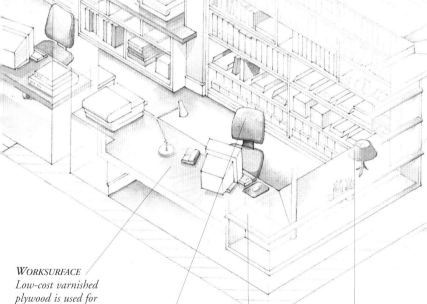

FOR MORE DETAILS...

Fitted desks SEE P. 26

Shelving SEE PP. 36–37

Natural light control
SEE PP. 38–39

Office technology
SEE PP. 42–43

WORKSURFACE
*Low-cost varnished
plywood is used for
the extensive fitted
worksurface.*

TASK CHAIRS
*All the task chairs match,
which helps to give the office
a sense of stylistic unity.*

L-SHAPED DESK
*The fitted desk turns the
corner, providing an
additional workspace.*

TABLE LAMP
*A small table lamp
provides soft, diffused
lighting.*

△ **❸ SERVICE AREA**
A partition separates the workstation from noisy
equipment in the lobby. The glass window lets in
light but not noise, and allows workers to check
incoming faxes from the main office area.

CONVERSION CHOICE

LOFT SKYLIGHT ▷
A skylight solves the double problem of lack of natural light and inadequate ventilation, common in loft conversions. For the best results, install the window with a blind directly above your working area.

▽ BEAMED CEILING
Converting an outhouse with original features does not mean that you have to continue the period look throughout the office. Here, exposed beamwork sits happily with modern office furniture.

△ ROOM WITH A VIEW
If you value an attractive outlook, install a picture window (one with no panes) to provide uninterrupted visual access to the outdoors.

◁ STUDY ROOM
An outhouse offers a peaceful place for work. This simply furnished room is painted in calming white, creating an almost monastic feel.

RURAL STUDIO ▷
The furniture in this converted stable enhances the rustic setting. The wooden floor matches the chest and chairs and the iron table legs complement the tethering post.

UNUSUAL SPACE OFFICE PLAN

CONSIDER UTILIZING DEAD SPACE in the house, such as a hallway or landing, if you cannot devote a room or part of a room to home-working. Here, a double-height kitchen offers the perfect opportunity for adding a mezzanine level for a small, open-plan office.

STURDY BASE
A metal beam is used to strengthen the plasterboard and timber platform.

Kitchen table   Shelves   Platform edge

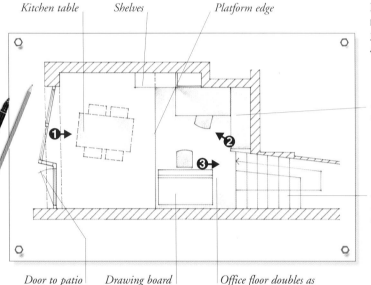

INTERNAL ROOM DIMENSIONS:
3m (9ft 10in) WIDE
4.3m (14ft) LONG

EXTENDED SPACE
Strong shelving extends beyond the platform to make the office space appear larger.

L-shaped worksurface

Half staircase to front door and rest of flat

Door to patio   Drawing board   Office floor doubles as kitchen ceiling

△ BIRD'S EYE PLAN
The mezzanine level projects out less than halfway across the kitchen area, allowing the dining area to enjoy the spaciousness of a double-height ceiling.

HEATING
A custom-made vertical radiator heats both floors.

DISCREET KITCHEN
Kitchen units are situated under the platform, which means that kitchen mess is invisible from the office.

WALL-TO-WALL WINDOWS
The double-height wall of windows and patio doors gives the office space excellent light and ample ventilation.

◁ ❶ ILLUSION OF SPACE
Although the office floor area is limited, the open design gives the room a feeling of space. The lack of a barrier at the edge of the office allows the eye to travel uninterrupted to its back.

FOR MORE DETAILS...

Drafting chair see p. 23

Natural light control see pp. 40–41

Workstation storage see pp. 34–35

ABLE CONTROL
he specially designed
sk has a cable duct
at carries cabling
wn the wall into
ckets.

LOW-LEVEL STORAGE
Built-in cupboards and shelves hold
regularly used reference material.

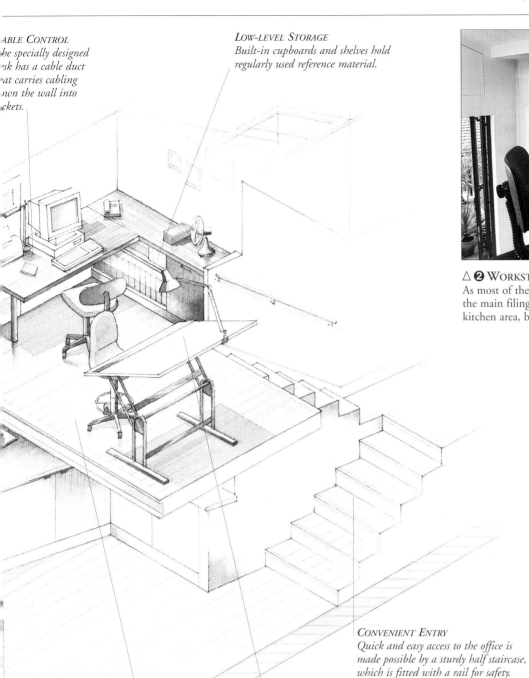

△ ❷ WORKSTATION STORAGE
As most of the floor space is taken up by worksurfaces, the main filing is held on shelves that project over the kitchen area, but are still within easy reach of the desk.

DESIGN POINTS

■ Seek professional advice before building a mezzanine floor. In particular, check local building regulations and load-bearing capabilities. Consult an architect for advice on a suitable space.

■ The installation of a half-height wall or safety railing is recommended on a mezzanine level, especially if the area is accessible to children or pets.

■ On a mezzanine level, additional wiring will almost certainly be required for power points and telephone sockets. Consult an electrician at the planning stage.

CONVENIENT ENTRY
Quick and easy access to the office is
made possible by a sturdy half staircase,
which is fitted with a rail for safety.

DRAWING BOARD
To enjoy maximum natural
light, the drawing board is
situated under the skylight.

MATCHING SURFACES
The timber floor is
painted to match the
worksurfaces and
kitchen units.

MEETING AREA
The dining table can
double up as a meeting
table when required.

❸ DIRECT ACCESS ▷
A staircase leads from the front door to the mezzanine level, allowing direct access to and from the office without entering the living space. Cabling is kept away from the stairs to prevent accidents.

UNUSUAL SPACE OFFICE CHOICE

△ TEMPORARY OFFICE
A stair landing is a suitable site for occasional work, although access to the staircase must always be kept clear for use as a fire escape. Here, the mobile desk and folding chair are easily removed if necessary. Remember, a landing can be noisy if other people are in the house.

◁ END OF HALLWAY
Dead space, often found at the end of a hallway, can be transformed into a compact office. The window makes this area a particularly attractive office. Such space may not be suitable if considerable storage facilities are required.

△ UNDERSTAIRS ALCOVE
Utilize the area under the staircase as an office for occasional work. Here, a freestanding table is used as a desk, though a fitted desk would work as well. Good artificial lighting is needed to compensate for the lack of natural light.

△ GALLERY SPACE
This large landing provides ample desk space and an area for meetings. A fitted desk with integral storage facilities takes little room, and the balcony allows in natural light. This is only a viable option in quiet houses.

IN SUSPENSION ▷
Dead air space in a stairwell is occupied here by an imaginatively designed suspended office. The wall, worksurface, and floor are constructed from toughened glass, allowing natural light to filter into the living space beneath.

EXECUTIVE OFFICE PLAN

IF RECEIVING AND IMPRESSING CLIENTS forms an important part of your work, you may require a formal, executive-type office. A spacious room is always impressive, though a small office can create the right ambience if it is well organized and equipped with stylish furniture and finishes. A crucial element is the provision of a desk or table for meetings with clients, which helps to set the businesslike tone of the office.

SOLID SCREEN
Solid-timber sliding doors provide good acoustic control between office and living area. The doors are top-hung, so the sliding mechanism is concealed when the doors are open.

MEETING CHAIRS
Leather chairs in the meeting/living area provide seating for both domestic living and informal meetings.

Entrance to flat · Sliding doors · Workstation · Fitted cupboards

TASK CHAIR
A high-backed, leather task chair signifies executive status.

Fireplace

Living room and meeting area · Workstation · Shelving

Window

△ **BIRD'S EYE VIEW**
Opening into the living room, which doubles as a meeting area, this large room comfortably contains two workstations.

INTERNAL ROOM DIMENSIONS:
5.5m (17ft 11in) WIDE
6.0m (19ft 6in) LONG

FITTED SHELVING
Adjustable shelves, made of medium-density fibreboard (MDF), hold books and files.

FLOORING
Pre-sealed oak laminate provides attractive, hard-wearing flooring.

COMFORT ZONE
The fireside rug helps to create the impression of a self-contained reading and rest area.

DESIGN POINTS

■ To prevent office noise penetrating to the floors above, or noises from above disturbing your work, insulate the ceiling with 100mm (4in) mineral fibre insulation.

■ The stylish look of an office can be ruined by power cables trailing across the floor. Avoid this by installing floor sockets directly under the workstation.

■ Lacquered finishes look luxurious but they chip easily, so avoid using them on areas of heavy use in your office.

◁ ❶ **EXECUTIVE DESK**
Providing a spacious workstation, this stylish large square desk, made of black lacquered wood with steel legs, has two pedestals that can be moved to make room for meetings of up to four people.

DISPLAY SPACE
*An entire wall has
been allocated for
displaying wall charts
and notice boards.*

❷ READING AREA ▷
A comfortable, leather easy chair and ottoman on a rug
by the fire create a cosy and relaxing reading area. The
space is well lit by a floorstanding downlighter and
natural light from the window, which is fitted with
electronically operated blinds.

WORKSTATION
*A second desk is situated near
filing cupboards and office
equipment, giving easy access
to frequently used material.*

STORAGE SURFACE
*The top surface of the cupboards
holds office equipment such as the
fax machine and printer.*

CUPBOARDS
*Ample storage for files is provided by
the run of white-painted cupboards,
which match the book shelves.*

WINDOW
*Sandblasted
industrial
glass blocks
are used for
the windows.*

FOR MORE DETAILS...

Executive high-back chair
SEE P. 23

Meeting areas SEE PP. 32–33

Surface finishes SEE PP. 44–45

Shelving SEE P. 37

FOCAL POINT
*A gas fire with realistic
flame effect warms the
entire space, both
visually and physically.*

FLEXIBLE FURNITURE
*A stacking stool doubles
as an occasional table or
plant stand.*

❸ ACCESS FROM THE LIVING AREA ▷
Two flush, sliding doors screen off the office from the
main living area. When the doors are open, the living
room becomes an extension of the office, providing a
large meeting area and letting light flow through from
the adjacent windows.

EXECUTIVE OFFICE CHOICE

△ GRAND BUT INFORMAL
The strikingly high ceiling and floor-to-ceiling windows make the most of natural light in this space. The focus of the office is the desk, which projects into the room and creates the impression that it is a centre of activity.

△ IMPOSING A STYLE
Think about your professional image, and how you would like to convey this to your clients. Here, the owner's idiosyncratic personality is reflected in the unusual and flamboyant furnishings and decor. The luxurious soft seating communicates to clients that their comfort is considered important.

△ MAKING A STATEMENT
If you live in a building with traditional features, and you want a modern style for your office, don't be afraid of placing contemporary furnishings within a conventional setting. Here, the glass worksurface, table lamp, leather chairs, and unusual wall display look at ease with the wood panelling.

CREATING FORMALITY ▷
One way to achieve a formal look is to use a traditional desk, which indicates the status of the owner and defines the relationship between the visitor and user. Remember that a large desk, while impressive, can also be intimidating.

PLOT YOUR DESIGN

PLOT YOUR ROOM

THE FLOOR PLAN and elevations are the starting point for any new office design. Use the following simple step-by-step guide to help you map out a survey of the room, and then to transfer your measurements to graph paper to create accurate scale drawings.

COLOURED PENCILS

RUBBER

NOTEPAD

CAMERA

STEP LADDER

TAPE MEASURE

EQUIPMENT
To help you create an accurate visual record of the room's dimensions, fixed service points, and awkward architectural features, you will need this basic equipment.

TAKING DIMENSIONS

As accurate measurements are vital to the success of your plan, take them with care. Note all details that will affect the positioning of furniture and equipment, such as the swing of the doors, the windows, and outside walls. Note all the radiators, switches, and power points, but don't be dictated by these as they can be moved to fit in with your final plan. Take photographs of the room throughout the day, so you can see how the sunlight changes, where it falls, and the areas that it never illuminates.

❶ **SKETCH THE ROOM**
Stand in the middle of the room and survey it, familiarizing yourself with each area. Draw a rough sketch of the room. Include any fixed features, such as fireplaces and alcoves, that will be incorporated into your final design.

❷ **PLOT THE DIMENSIONS**
Next, measure the total floor area: its length and width. It may be worth measuring diagonally, as walls are not always square, particularly in old buildings or conversions. Take the measurements of alcoves and other fixed features.

❸ **PLOT THE WALLS**
Working your way around the room in a clockwise direction, measure each wall length in turn. Do not assume that the walls are symmetrical. Carefully mark down all the measurements on your room sketch for future reference.

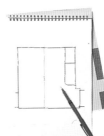

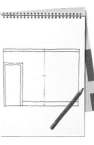

❹ **PLOT FIXED FEATURES**
Measure the dimensions of any structural or fixed items such as fireplaces and built-in furniture. Decide if you want to move any of these features. Take a note of the service points such as radiators and power points that you may want moved.

❺ **MEASURE THE HEIGHT**
Stand facing each wall in turn and draw a sketch of it. Draw in the doors, windows, alcoves, and any architectural details which may restrict the height of shelving. Stand on a step ladder and measure the wall height from floor to ceiling.

❻ **MEASURE THE DOORS**
On each wall sketch, note the height and width of the doors, skirtings, and any surrounding frames or mouldings. Note the way the door and windows open. Photograph areas that are difficult to measure, such as corners.

DRAWING UP SCALE PLANS

The rough sketch survey of the existing room plan (*see p.76*) contains basic information to help you work out where to place your workstation, active, passive, and remote storage, and information technology equipment, and what space you may have left for a meeting area or soft seating. However, if you wish to take the design further, you may want to draw up the plan and elevations to scale. Follow the instructions below to help you experiment with different ideas for creating your ideal home office.

YOU WILL NEED
Metric and imperial graph paper is supplied with this book but you will also need a set square, ruler, sharp pencil, and ink pen.

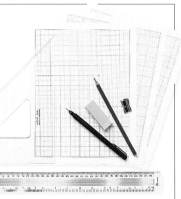

TRANSFER THE FLOOR PLAN ▷
Refer to your rough plan for precise measurements, and then accurately plot the four perimeter walls to scale on graph paper. Remember to include diagonal dimensions in order to account for any asymmetry in the room. Join up the straight lines with a set square. Plot features such as outside walls, doors, and windows. Add the position of services such as radiators and power points.

▽ DRAW UP THE ELEVATIONS
Referring to the measurements on your room sketch, draw up each wall to scale. Work from the floor upwards, marking on details and services last. First outline the cornices and skirting board in a thicker line. Add the main fixed features, such as windows, doors, and fireplaces. In a lighter pencil, fill in details of architectural mouldings around the windows and door, the direction the windows and the door open, and the radiators. Add the dimensions around the outside of the drawing, so the elevations do not become cluttered.

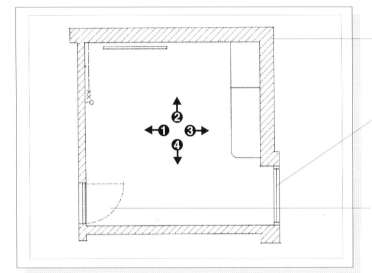

OUTSIDE WALLS
A thick border of cross-hatching indicates outside walls.

LIGHT
Parallel lines show a window as a light source.

DOOR HINGING
A dotted line indicates the way in which the door opens.

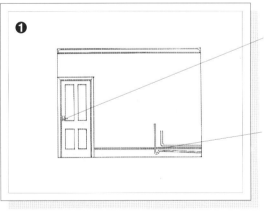

① DOOR KNOB
Indicate the side the door opens by drawing on the door handle.

WATER PIPES
Mark the position of services, such as water pipes.

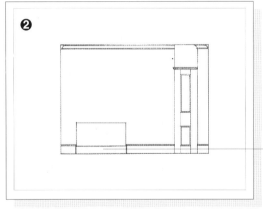

② THE WHOLE PICTURE
For accuracy, draw in the radiator, skirting board, and the side of a cupboard seen from this viewpoint.

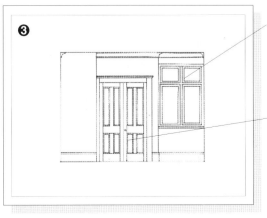

③ WINDOWS
Include details such as moulding and windowsill measurements.

CUPBOARD
The position of the cupboard is indicated, even though it is to be moved to another room.

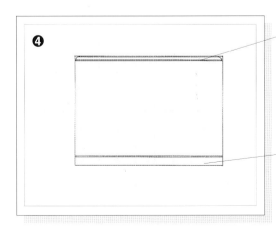

④ CORNICE HEIGHT
The width of the cornice will limit the height of tall shelves.

SKIRTING BOARD
A thicker line distinguishes the skirting board from the floor line.

PLACE THE FEATURES

BEGIN BY COMPILING A LIST of all the furniture, equipment, storage requirements, and other features that you wish to include in your office, bearing in mind the kind of work you do and its specific needs, as well as your personal preferences. The next step is to find a successful way of organizing these elements in your work space. Following the Order of Design (*see right*), try out different arrangements by placing a piece of tracing paper over the scaled-up room plan (*see pp.76–77*), and drawing on the elements. You may have to draw several versions before you reach the best solution.

YOU WILL NEED ▷
Place a sheet of tracing paper over your floor plan scale drawing, holding both securely in position with masking tape. Using a soft pencil, ruler, and set square, draw in your listed features in possible locations. Start each new design on a clean sheet of tracing paper.

MASKING TAPE

TRACING PAPER

SET SQUARE

PEN
PENCIL
RUBBER

RULER

ORDER OF DESIGN

When designing your home office, place your chosen components on the room plan in the following order.

❶ **WORKSTATION** Your workstation forms the hub of your office, with other elements planned around it. Proximity to a natural light source and the position of your computer screen are the key considerations.

❷ **ACTIVE STORAGE** of constantly used files, equipment, and stationery should be within an arm's reach of the workstation.

❸ **PASSIVE STORAGE** of less frequently used items, such as shelves and filing cabinets, can be further away from the workstation.

❹ **MEETING AREA** Select a space that is further from the window than the desk, and with a nearby wall for presentation material.

❺ **REST AREA** A comfortable chair placed close to the workstation or in a quiet reading area serves as a visitor's chair as well as a place for you to read, think, or relax.

REJECTED PLANS

It takes time to arrive at a well-designed, ergonomic plan, especially if your work space contains fixed features that have to be incorporated into the design. Let your plan evolve and learn, in the process, from the designs that you reject.

UNRESOLVED AREAS ▽
In this plan, which makes little use of natural light and leaves two corners unresolved, the meeting area dominates the space, while the active storage area is too far from the desk.

SOFT SEATING
Although close to the desk, the chair is tucked away in an unattractive corner space.

DESK AREA
The desk faces the wall opposite the window, which may create shadows and glare on the screen.

PASSIVE STORAGE
Shelving along this wall partially obscures light from the window.

ACTIVE STORAGE
Frequently used items are not within easy reach of the task chair.

MEETING AREA
This area is closer to the window than the desk, and has no nearby wall for presentation material.

POOR ACCESS TO STORAGE ▽
Though the desk is now closer to the window, with more natural light and partial views, it is isolated from the active storage area on the opposite side of the room, beyond the meeting table, which holds regularly used files and equipment.

PASSIVE STORAGE
In this plan, passive storage is closer to the desk than the active storage area.

DESK FACING WALL
Although the desk is now close to the window, the space between it and the meeting area is cramped.

WASTED SPACE
Although this corner benefits from natural light, its use remains unresolved.

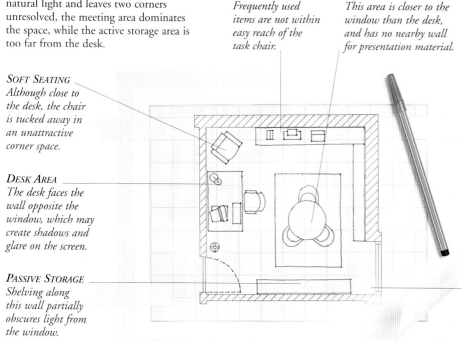

SUCCESSFUL PLAN

Having carefully explored the possibilities and found the most effective and pleasing way of arranging the elements in your work space, you can now plot your final design on graph paper.

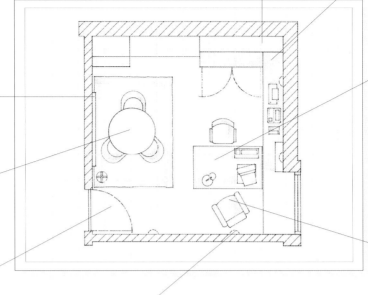

PASSIVE STORAGE
A visually harmonious, single wall of storage can be reached without any obstructions, and is relatively close to the task area.

ACTIVE STORAGE
Fax, printer, and files are within arm's reach of the desk and can be accessed by swivelling the task chair.

PRESENTATION WALL
A wall with good natural light, immediately behind the meeting area, provides a useful surface for displaying presentation material.

DESK
Although the desk is not directly in front of the window, it is close enough to benefit from the natural light. It is positioned at right angles to prevent glare on the computer monitor.

MEETING AREA
The meeting table and chairs are conveniently situated, without obstructing other elements.

SOFT SEATING
Out of the way of traffic areas, the easy chair gets good natural light and can double as a meeting chair for single visitors.

ENTRANCE DOOR
The whole work area can be viewed from the door, which is unobstructed by furniture.

LIGHTING
Wall lights are placed on the available wall space around the main work area to provide ambient lighting, which complements the desktop task light.

ACTIVE STORAGE
This area is too far from the desk for frequently used files and equipment, such as fax and printer.

UNUSED CENTRAL SPACE ▽
The desk is in the darkest area of the room, with no view, although it is closer to the active storage area than in the previous plan. All the elements have been arranged around the walls, leaving a large, central area of dead space.

ACTIVE STORAGE
Although closer than in previous plans, the active storage area is still too far from the desk.

DESK IN THE DARK
As well as being in the darkest area of the room, the desk uses up valuable wall space.

MEETING AREA
The centrally placed meeting table obstructs movement from the desk to the active storage area.

SOFT SEATING
Placed here, the chair impedes access to storage and clutters space.

PASSIVE STORAGE
Shelving for passive storage is closer to the desk than the provision for more frequently used items.

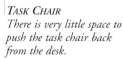

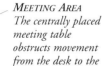

TASK CHAIR
There is very little space to push the task chair back from the desk.

ENTRANCE DOOR
Access is restricted by shelving and by the meeting area.

MEETING AREA
The benefit of natural light is wasted on a meeting area that is used only occasionally.

SOFT SEATING
Placed here, the chair blocks easy movement around the meeting area.

PLANNING DETAIL

ONCE YOU HAVE DECIDED on the most suitable floor plan, you can begin to consider the details. Choose flooring, lighting, shelving, and cabinet finishes that coordinate with your desk, task chair, and overall style. Bear in mind any budget constraints and the potential for future expansion.

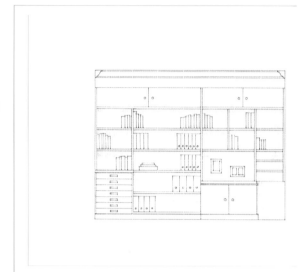

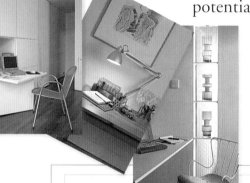

◁ **COLLECT PHOTOGRAPHS**
To help you choose furniture and finishes for your new office, and to help you clarify your preferred style – whether traditional, modern, or hi-tech – start collecting pictures from magazines and catalogues.

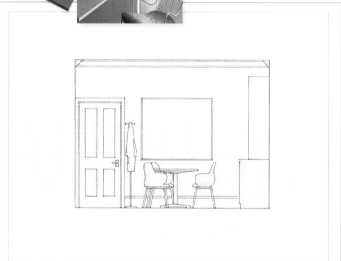

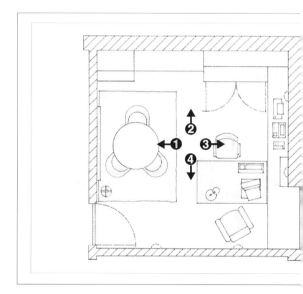

△ ❶ **MEETING TABLE AND PRESENTATION BOARD**
A round meeting table is most space-efficient, but make sure that there is enough room for chairs to be pushed back without scraping the wall. Fix the presentation board at a height suited to those sitting at the table, and provide a freestanding or wall-hung coat rack.

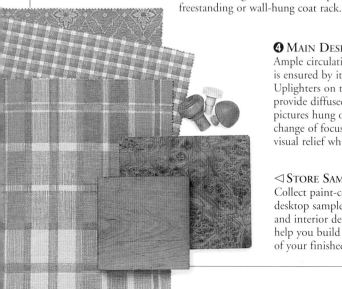

❹ **MAIN DESK AND WALL LIGHTS** ▷
Ample circulation space around the desk is ensured by its distance from the door. Uplighters on the wall facing the desk provide diffused ambient light, while pictures hung on the same wall provide a change of focus for the eyes, to give some visual relief while working.

◁ **STORE SAMPLES**
Collect paint-colour, tile, and desktop samples from DIY and interior design shops to help you build up a picture of your finished office.

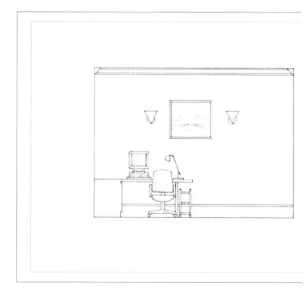

REFER TO CATALOGUES ▷
Keep the catalogues that feature
your choice of furniture
and materials: they will
help you to cost the project
and check dimensions, as
well as providing addresses of
local stockists and suppliers.

◁ **❷ PASSIVE STORAGE AREA**
Maximize the use of space by covering a
whole wall with cupboards and shelving,
but make sure that the shelves are wide
enough for your files, and that drawers
are placed no higher than waist height.
Conceal stationery and unsightly clutter
in built-in cupboards, which can also
provide additional worksurfaces.

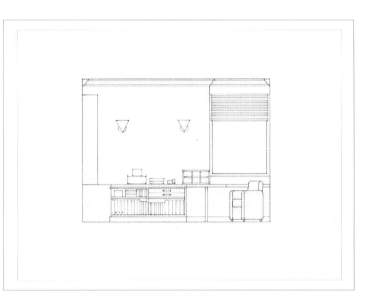

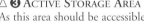

▷ **FLOOR PLAN**
A bird's eye view shows
you exactly how the office
elements are placed in
relation to the shape of
the room.

△ **❸ ACTIVE STORAGE AREA**
As this area should be accessible by swivelling
round in your task chair, make sure the shelving
is placed at the correct height – approximately
750mm (29in). The worksurface will be in
constant use and must hold heavy equipment,
so should be well constructed, with a
durable surface.

△ **LIGHT FITTINGS**
After drawing up your
lighting plan, arrange
for wiring work to be
carried out before you
install cabinets or start
to decorate. Make sure
the plan provides
adequate lighting for
the main work area.

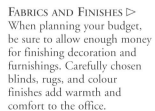

FABRICS AND FINISHES ▷
When planning your budget,
be sure to allow enough money
for finishing decoration and
furnishings. Carefully chosen
blinds, rugs, and colour
finishes add warmth and
comfort to the office.

WHAT NEXT?

■ If you are opting for system
furniture, take your finished
design to an office furniture
supplier who will check
your plans and advise you
on which system will best
suit your requirements.

■ Obtain planning permission
from the relevant authorities
for structural alterations,
conversions, or the creation
of new windows.

■ Coordination of work is
important, so agree a schedule
with everybody involved. The
sequence of work is as follows:
structural alterations, wiring
and plumbing, floor laying,
base-coat decoration, fitting
shelves, final electrical
and decorating work.

■ Check that delivery dates
for furniture and materials
meet your work schedule.

■ If you already work at
home, set up a temporary
office that will allow you
to work away from the
noise of the builders until the
alterations are complete.

BUDGET TIPS

■ To calculate the cost of your
new office, obtain estimates
for all the building, plumbing,
and electrical work that has to
be done. Add to this the cost
of all new furniture,
equipment, shelving, and
finishes that you have chosen.

■ If your ideal office plan is
beyond your budget, look at
ways of cutting costs – opting
for laminate rather than solid
wood flooring; making a desk
rather than buying one;
choosing cheaper
fittings or finishes.

■ Allow a small contingency
to cover unexpected costs,
particularly if you are having
structural work carried out.

STOCKISTS AND SUPPLIERS

The following directory of useful names and addresses will help you source the shops needed to furnish and equip your home office. The letters (*MO*) after an entry indicate that items are available by mail order; some retailers may operate a mail order service as well as selling through a shop (*Also available MO*). If you are considering structural work, it is advisable to consult an architect.

ARCHITECTS

RIBA
Client Advisory Service
66 Portland Place
London W1N 4AD
Tel: 0171 307 3700
Offers free service recommending local architects.

ALLFORD HALL MONAGHAN MORRIS
23c Old Street
London EC1V 9HL
Tel: 0171 251 5261

BIRDS PORTCHMOUTH RUSSUM
9 Hatton Street
London NW8 8PL
Tel: 0171 724 1505

CANY ASH AND ROBERT SAKULA
Studio 115
38 Mount Pleasant
London WC1N 2PG
Tel: 0171 837 9735

GRAVEN IMAGES
83a Candleriggs
Glasgow G1 1LF
Tel: 0141 552 6626

MARY THUM ASSOCIATES
30 Carlyle Square
London SW3 6HA
Tel: 0171 376 8996

STUDIO MG ARCHITECTS
101 Turnmill Street
London EC1M 5QP
Tel: 0171 251 5261

GENERAL

ATRIUM LTD
Centrepoint
22–24 St Giles High Street
London WC2H 8LN
Tel: 0171 379 7288
Stockists of a small range of stylish desks and chairs and light fittings.

THE BACK SHOP
14 New Cavendish Street
London W1M 7LJ
Tel: 0171 935 9120
Wide selection of specialist seating and accessories to encourage good posture and combat back problems.

COEXISTENCE
288 Upper Street
London N1 2TZ
Tel: 0171 354 8817
Contemporary furniture and accessories.

THE CONRAN SHOP
Michelin House
81 Fulham Road
London SW3 6RD
Tel: 0171 589 7401
Office furniture and accessories.

HABITAT (HEAD OFFICE)
196 Tottenham Court Road
London W1P 9LD
Tel: 0171 255 2545 for local branches
Good selection of middle-price range home office furniture.

HEAL'S
196 Tottenham Court Road
London W1P 9LD
Tel: 0171 636 1666
Range of contemporary furniture and accessories.

INHOUSE
28 Howe Street
Edinburgh EH3 6TG
Tel: 0131 225 2888
Designer furniture.

IKEA
Ikea Tower
255 North Circular Road
London NW10 0JQ
Tel: 0181 233 2300 for details of local stores
Good selection of self-assemble low-cost desks and storage units.

JOHN LEWIS PARTNERSHIP
278–306 Oxford Street
London W1 1EX
Tel: 0171 629 7711 for local branches
Range of furniture and accessories.

LOFT CENTRE PRODUCTS
Quarry Lane Industrial Estates
Chichester
West Sussex PO19 2NY
Tel: 01243 785246
Loft ladders and space-saving stairs.

NICE HOUSE
The Italian Centre
Ingram Street
Glasgow G1 1HD
Tel: 0141 553 1377
Contemporary designer lamps and seating.

THE PIER
200 Tottenham Court Road
London W1P 0AD
Tel: 0171 637 7001 for local branches
Selection of stacking baskets and folding chairs.

PURVES & PURVES
See Accessories

RJ'S HOME SHOP
209 Tottenham Court Road
London W1P 9AF
Tel: 0171 637 7474
Low-cost home office furniture and accessories.

VIADUCT FURNITURE LTD
1–10 Summers Street
London EC1R 5BD
Tel: 0171 278 8456
High-quality Italian, French, and Spanish designer furniture.

OFFICE & HOME OFFICE FURNITURE

BEAVER AND TAPLEY
Scotts Road
Southall
Middlesex UB2 5DJ
Tel: 0181 574 4311
Versatile self-assembly, fitted and freestanding office furniture.

BROADAKER COMPANY LTD
Church Road
St Sampsons
Guernsey GY2 4LW
Tel: 01481 46818 for details
of local stockists
*Manufacturers of Pivotelli
wall-mounted adjustable
stands for computers.*

BULO OFFICE FURNITURE
The Clove Building
Maguire Street
Butler's Wharf
London SE1 2NQ
Tel: 0171 403 6993
Contemporary desks and storage units.

CASTLE GIBSON
106A Upper Street
London N1 1QN
Tel: 0171 704 0927
Range of secondhand traditional office furniture.

THE DESIGN & PRODUCTION GROUP
The Hat Factory
16–18 Hollen Street
London W1V 3AD
Tel: 0171 437 5060
*Contemporary home office desk designed
for computers and accessories.*

ESTIA COMPONENT FURNITURE
Factory Showroom
Unit 1
Enterprise Works
Lockfield Avenue
Enfield EN3 7PX
Tel: 0171 636 5957
Modular desk and storage systems.

GEOFFREY DRAYTON
85 Hampstead Road
London NW1 2BL
Tel: 0171 387 5840
Several ranges of home office furniture.

HAWORTH UK LTD
10 New Oxford Street
London WC1A 1EE
Tel: 0171 404 1617
Complete office units.

HERMAN MILLER
149 Tottenham Court Road
London W1P 0JA
Tel: 0171 388 7331
*Sophisticated home office desks, screens, and
storage systems.*

IKEA
See General

INTERLÜBKE LONDON
Tel: 0171 207 4710 for
details of local stockists
*Bookcases, cabinets, and home
office storage.
(Also available MO)*

JUST DESKS OFFICE INTERIORS
20 Church Street
London NW8 8EP
Tel: 0171 723 7976
*Reproduction computer desks, bureaux, and
reception units.*

KNOLL INTERNATIONAL
1 East Market
Lindsay Street
London EC1A 9PQ
Tel: 0171 236 6655
High-quality computer desks and task chairs.

MARCATRE
143–149 Great Portland Street
London W1N 5FB
Tel: 0171 436 1808
*Contemporary office and home office furniture;
good selection of computer desks.*

NEWCASTLE FURNITURE COMPANY
128 Walham Green Court
Moore Park Road
London SW6 4DG
Tel: 0171 386 9203
*Shaker-style, high-quality home office desks and
units.*

OFFICE WORLD
339 The Hyde
Edgware Road
London NW9 6TH
Tel: 0181 205 4466 for local branches
Large selection of office furniture and equipment.

SASHA WADDELL
Kingshill Designs
Kitchener Road
High Wycombe
Bucks HP11 2SJ
Tel: 01494 463910
*Home office furniture modelled on
traditional Swedish design.*

SCP LTD
135–139 Curtain Road
London EC2A 3BX
Tel: 0171 739 1869
Contemporary desks and shelving.

POWERDESK PLC
Broyle Place Industrial Estate
Laughton Road
Ringmer
East Sussex BN8 5SD
Tel: 01273 814824
Desks in various styles with integral PC.

RICHARD KIMBELL
Units 1 and 2
Coombe Square
Chapel Street
Thatcham
Berkshire RG19 4JF
Tel: 01635 874822
Country-style complete home office unit.

ROCHE BOBOIS
421–425 Finchley Road
London NW3 6HJ
Tel: 0171 431 1411
*Traditional-style desks and
shelving.*

VITRA UK LIMITED
13 Grosvenor Street
London W1X 9FB
Tel: 0171 408 1122
*High-quality ergonomic office seating and
range of home office furniture.*

FITTED OFFICES

CHRISTIES
First Avenue
Royal Portbury Dock Estate
Portbury
Bristol BS20 9XP
Tel: 01275 378000
*Custom-designed fitted studies and
dual-purpose office/bedrooms.*

NEVILLE JOHNSON
Broadoak Business Park
Ashburton Road West
Trafford Park
Manchester M17 1RW
Tel: 0161 873 8333
Custom-designed fitted offices.

LIGHTING

ATRIUM LTD
See General

CAZ SYSTEMS
19 Church Street
Brighton BN1 IUS
Tel: 01273 326471
Contemporary light fittings.

CHRISTOPHER WRAY LIGHTING
591–593 King's Road
London SW6 2YW
Tel: 0171 736 8434
Wide selection of light fittings for the home.

CONCORD LIGHTING
174 High Holborn
London WC1V 7AA
Tel: 0171 497 1400
Wide range of modern light fittings.

ERCO
38 Dover Street
London W1X 3RB
Tel: 0171 408 0320
Spot and ambient office-related lighting.

FLOS
(British Showroom)
31 Lisson Grove
London NW1 6UV
Tel: 0171 258 0660
Wide selection of designer lighting.

THE LONDON LIGHTING COMPANY
135 Fulham Road
London SW3 6RT
Tel: 0171 589 3612
Good selection of light fittings for the home.

RETROUVIUS
32 York House
Upper Montagu Street
London W1H 1FR
Tel: 0171 402 6826
Contemporary lighting and architectural design.

SHIU KAY KAN
Lexington Street
London W1R 3HR
Tel: 0171 434 4095
Wide selection of contemporary lighting.

BLINDS, SHUTTERS, SCREENS, AND CURTAINS

ALISON WHITE
Ground Floor
Fitzpatrick Building
York Way
London N7 9AS
Tel: 0171 609 6127
Solid and translucent screens, perforated blinds, and lighting.

THE FINAL CURTAIN COMPANY
Tel: 0181 699 3626 (workroom)
Curtains to order.

THE LONDON SHUTTER CO
18 Brockenhurst Road
Ascot
Berkshire SL5 9DL
Tel: 01344 28385
Custom-made internal, cedarwood shutters.

THE NATURAL HOME SHOP
387 Manchester Road
Heaton Chapel
Stockport
Cheshire SK4 5BY
Tel: 0161 442 1400
Roman, sheer, and micro blinds.

THE SHUTTER SHOP
Queensbury House
Dilly Lane
Hartley Wintney
Hampshire RG27 8EQ
Tel: 0171 229 9095
Custom-made interior shutters with adjustable louvres.

SILENTGLISS LTD
Star Lane
Margate
Kent CT9 4EF
Tel: 01843 863571
High-quality blinds, curtains, and space dividers.

TIDMARSH & SONS
1 Laycock Street,
London N1 1SW
Tel: 0171 226 2261
High-quality venetian blinds.

STORAGE

ALLSTEEL
Innsbruck House
9–11 Garden Walk
London EC2A 3EQ
Tel: 0171 613 4000
Storage systems and lateral files in a wide range of attractive colours.

BISLEY OFFICE FURNITURE
FC Brown (Steel Equipment) Ltd
Queens Road
Bisley
Surrey GU24 9BJ
Tel: 01483 474577
Inexpensive storage systems and pedestals.

THE CUBESTORE
38 Grosvenor Road
London W4 4EG
Tel: 0181 944 6016
Modular cube storage systems. (MO)

THE HOLDING COMPANY
243–245 King's Road
London SW3 5EL
Tel: 0171 352 1600
Wide range of storage accessories, including cable control devices. (Also available MO)

HOMEBASE LTD (HEAD OFFICE)
Beddington House
Wallington
Surrey SM6 0HB
Tel: 0181 784 7200 for details of local stores
Low-cost shelving for self assembly.

I. PALMER & SONS
106–110 Lower Parliament Street
Nottingham NG1 1EH
Tel: 0115 950 4787
Storage boxes made to order. (MO)

THE MAINE GROUP
Facilit Group
Riverside Gallery
2 O&N Metropolitan Wharf
Wapping Wall
London E1 9SS
Tel: 0171 480 7642
Filing cabinets in a range of colours.

OCEAN HOME SHOPPING LTD
PO Box 7837
London SW15 1ZA
Tel: 0800 132985
Storage boxes and accessories. (MO)

SPUR SHELVING
Otterspool Way
Watford
Hertforshire WD2
8QT
Tel: 01923 226071 for
details of local stockists
*Wide range of shelving
systems.*

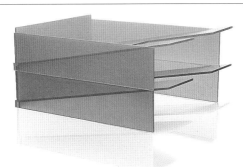

DESK SURFACES AND FLOORING

AMTICO
18 Hanover Square
London W1R 9BD
Tel: 0171 629 6258
High-quality vinyl flooring and laminates.

CHRISTOPHER FARR
212 Westbourne Grove
London W11 2RH
Tel: 0171 792 5761
Contemporary hand-tufted rugs.

DOMUS TILES
33 Parkgate Road
London SW11 4NP
Tel: 0171 223 5555
High-quality Italian ceramic tiles.

FORBO-NAIRN (HEAD OFFICE)
PO Box 1
Kircaldy
Fife KY1 2SB
Tel: 01592 643777
High-quality linoleum and vinyl sheets and tiles.

FORMICA LTD
Coast Road
North Shields
Tyne and Wear NE29 8RE
Tel: 0191 259 3000
Laminated worktops.

HARGREAVES FLOORING LTD
Unit 6
Granary Square Business Park
Falkirk FK2 7XJ
Tel: 01324 611152
*Hardwood, natural fibre, linoleum, and cork
flooring.*

JUNKERS
Wheaton Court
Commercial Centre
Wheaton Road
Whitham
Essex CMB 3UJ
Tel: 01376 517 512
Hardwood flooring.

ACCESSORIES

AERO
96 Westbourne
Grove
London W2 5RT
Tel: 0171 221 1950
*Furniture and desk
accessories.*
(Also available MO)

CAZ SYSTEMS
See Lighting

DESIGNERS GUILD
261–271 & 277 King's Road
London SW3 5EN
Tel: 0171 351 5775
Desk accessories.
(Also available MO)

THE GENERAL TRADING COMPANY
144 Sloane Street
London SW1X 9BL
Tel: 0171 730 0411
Desk accessories.
(Also available MO)

MUJI
26 Great Marlborough Street
London W1V 1HL
Tel: 0171 494 1197
Storage, shelves, desk accessories, and stationery.

PAPERCHASE
213 Tottenham Court Road
London W1P 2AF
Tel: 0171 580 8496 for details of
nearest branch
Storage accessories and stationery.
(Also available MO)

PURVES & PURVES
80–81 & 83 Tottenham Court Road
London W1P 9HD
Tel: 0171 580 8223
Contemporary furniture and accessories.

RUTH ARRAM SHOP
65 Heath Street
London NW3 6UG
Tel: 0171 431 4008
Contemporary accessories.

RYMAN
Ryman House,
Swallowfield Way
Hayes
Middlesex UB3 1DQ
Tel: 01372 813388 for
details of nearest branch
Stationery and furniture.

SMYTHSON OF BOND STREET
44 New Bond Street
London W1X 0DE
Tel: 0171 629 8558
Traditional stationery and desk accessories.

VIKING DIRECT LTD
Bursom Industrial Park
Tollwell Road
Leicester LE4 1BR
Tel: 0990 340 404
*Low-cost office furniture, equipment, stationery,
and accessories. (MO)*

IT EQUIPMENT

CAMELOT
Unit 2
10 William Road
London NW1 3EN
Tel: 0171 383 2727
*Authorized reseller of AppleMac and other
computer hardware.*

COMPUTER WAREHOUSE
9 Hatton Street
London NW8 8PR
Tel: 0171 724 3775
*Authorized reseller of AppleMac and other
computer hardware.*

MACWAREHOUSE
Dept C, Unit 6
Wolsey Park
Tolpits Lane
Watford WD1 8QP
Tel: 0990 275405
Authorized reseller of AppleMac and other

TELEWORKING ASSOCIATIONS

BRITISH TELECOM
*How to use information technology and new
communications to help your work.*
Tel: 0800 800844

**THE TELECOTTAGE
ASSOCIATION**
WREN Telecottage
Stoneleigh Park
Warwickshire CV8 2RR
Tel: 0800 616008
*Courses and information on
computers and teleworking.*

NEW WAYS TO WORK
309 Upper Street
London N1 2TY
Tel: 0171 226 4026
Advice on flexible working.

INDEX

ACKNOWLEDGMENTS

AUTHOR'S ACKNOWLEDGMENTS

I would like to thank all those who allowed us to trample into their home offices, to disrupt their work, and to cross-examine them. My grateful thanks to the talented architects whose ingenious yet practical work we have used; their generous cooperation made this book possible: Cany Ash and Robert Sakula, Mary Thum, John Grimes, and Mike Russum.

Special thanks are due to Simon Allford and Paul Monaghan of Allford Hall Monaghan Morris whose design skills are well-demonstrated in their stunning home-office projects and who helped to source other examples, a difficult task in a new area. Their patience and advice was much appreciated.

Thanks to the dedicated team at Dorling Kindersley for their hard work and enthusiasm. In particular, thanks to Mary-Clare Jerram for commissioning me and for her support, to Charlotte Davies, Martin Lovelock, Clive Hayball, and Susie Behar for their humour and patience.

Thanks also to Jeremy Myerson for his encouragement, Paul Simmons and Eve Gaventa for their support, and finally to Dominic Papa for all his advice and expertise, and design skills.

PUBLISHER'S ACKNOWLEDGMENTS

Dorling Kindersley would like to thank: Ally Ireson for picture research; Robert Campbell for technical support; Hilary Bird for the index; Martin Hendry, Alan McKee, Sharon Moore, John Round, and Colin Walton for design assistance; Irene Lyford for editorial assistance; Richard Hammond for proof-reading; and Jessica Rettallaek for prop buying.

We would like to thank the architects whose plans appear in the book: Allford Hall Monaghan Morris 70–71; Birds Portchmouth Russum 66–67; Cany Ash and Robert Sakula 62–63; Studio MG Architects 58–59; Mary Thum Associates 54–55.

We are indebted to the following individuals who generously allowed us to photograph in their homes: Simon Fanshawe; Martin Lovelock; Chris Riddell; David and Issy Simmonds; Simon Webb and Jess Walton.

We would like to thank the following companies for allowing us to photograph in their showrooms: Atrium 24bc, 25tc, 27lc; Co-existence 33tr, 234br; Haworth 30b; Herman Miller 23tc, 30 ct, 35tr, 36bc; Just Desks 29bc; Marcatre 28tc, 28bc, 26b.

We would also like to thank the following individuals and companies who lent us items for photography: Aero 20, 21; The Back Shop 23tr; Sebastian Bergne 85tl, 87tc; Bond Street Carpets 44br, 45b; Nel Brett 41tr, 48; Caz Systems; The Chelsea Gardener; The Holding Company 43cr, 47bl, 87br; Clare Mosely Gilding 46br; Nicholas; Primrose and Primrose; Retro Homestores 47br; RJ's HomeShop 36tl; Gillian Roberts 41tc; Shiu-Kay Kan; Gerard Taylor; Vitra.

ARTWORK

David Ashby 22, 26, 29, 38, 40; Richard Lee 50–51, 54–55, 58–59, 62–63, 66–67, 70–71, 74–75, 76–77, 78–79, 80–81.

PHOTOGRAPHY

All photographs by Peter Anderson and Andy Crawford, except:
Abode/Ian Parry (Marjorie McDougall) 27tl; Otto Baitz/Esto 38t, 68br; Reiner Blunck/Marie Claire Maison/Jean-Pierre Godeaut (J.P. Billaud) 42tl; Brigitte/Camera Press 34l, 37tl, 56tl, 56bc; Jeremy Cockayne/Arcaid 57; Mark Darley/Esto (architect: Brenda Levine) 64cr; Christopher Drake/Options/Robert Harding Syndication 7; Jake Fitzjones 60bl; Dennis Gilbert/Arcaid (architects: Allford Hall Monaghan Morris) 69; Jeff Goldberg/Esto (Nancy Levine and Rita Marks) 26cl; Living/Camera Press 68bl; Ray Main 60tl; Marie Claire Maison/Nicolas Tosi (J. Borgeaud) 40tl; Derry Moore courtesy of Architectural Digest 6tl, 6b; Michael Nicholson/Elizabeth Whiting and Associates 24br; The Interior Archive/Tim Clinch 46cl; Paul Ryan/International Interiors 32l (architect: Korinne Kalesso), 52tl (designer: Maeve Mougin), 52b (architect: Ian Hay), 53 (designer: Sam Blount), 56bl (designer: Sasha Waddell), 61 (Wolfgang Joop); SchonerWohnen/Camera Press 31br, 60tr, 64b, 68tl; Solvi Dos Santos 13, 52tr, 72tl, 72b, 73; Fritz von der Schulenburg/The Interior Archive 72tr; Ian Skelton/Homes & Ideas/Robert Harding Syndication 25br; Tim Street-Porter/Elizabeth Whiting and Associates (designer: Lloyd Ziff) 64cl; Colin Walton 24tr, 74, 78bl, c, 79br, 80bl, br.

The following companies kindly lent us photographs: Ikea Ltd 56ct; Newcastle Furniture Company 31tr, 31tl; Neville Johnson Fitted Furniture/GGT Direct 64t; Nice House 14br, 37br; Silent Gliss 33br; Vitra 9tr, 27br, 22, 23tl.

Every effort has been made to trace the copyright holders. We apologise for any omission and would be pleased to insert these in subsequent editions.

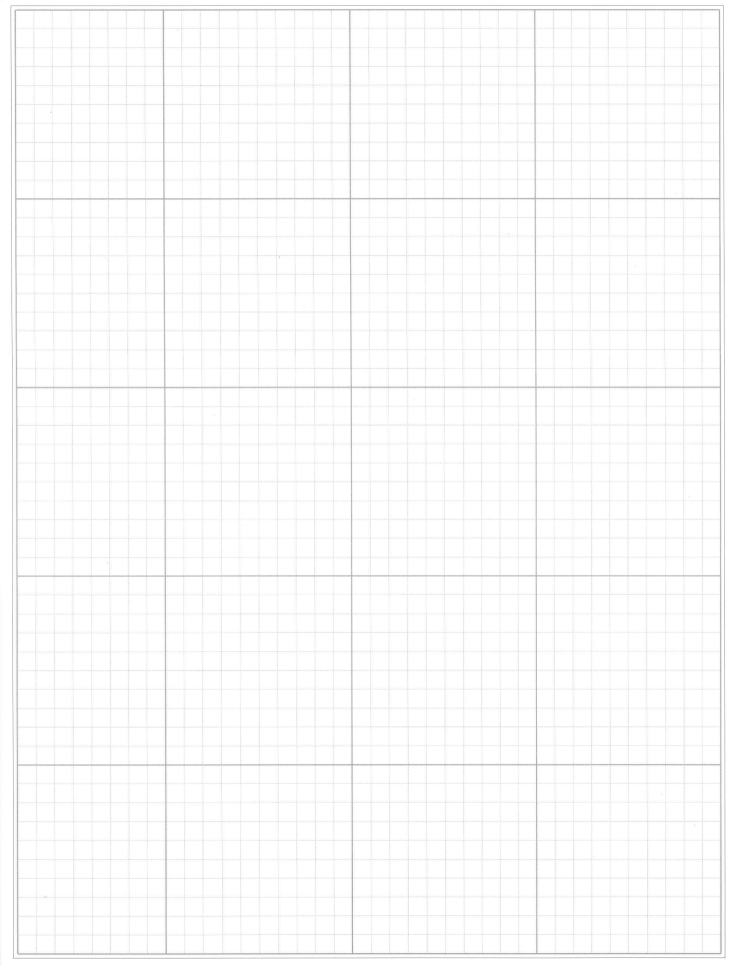

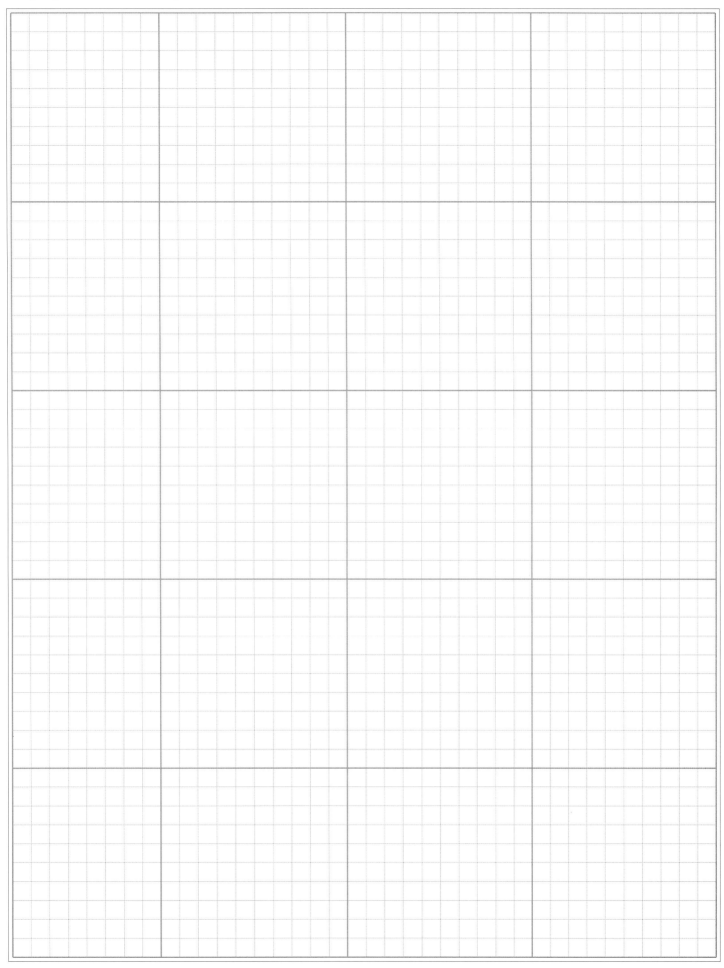

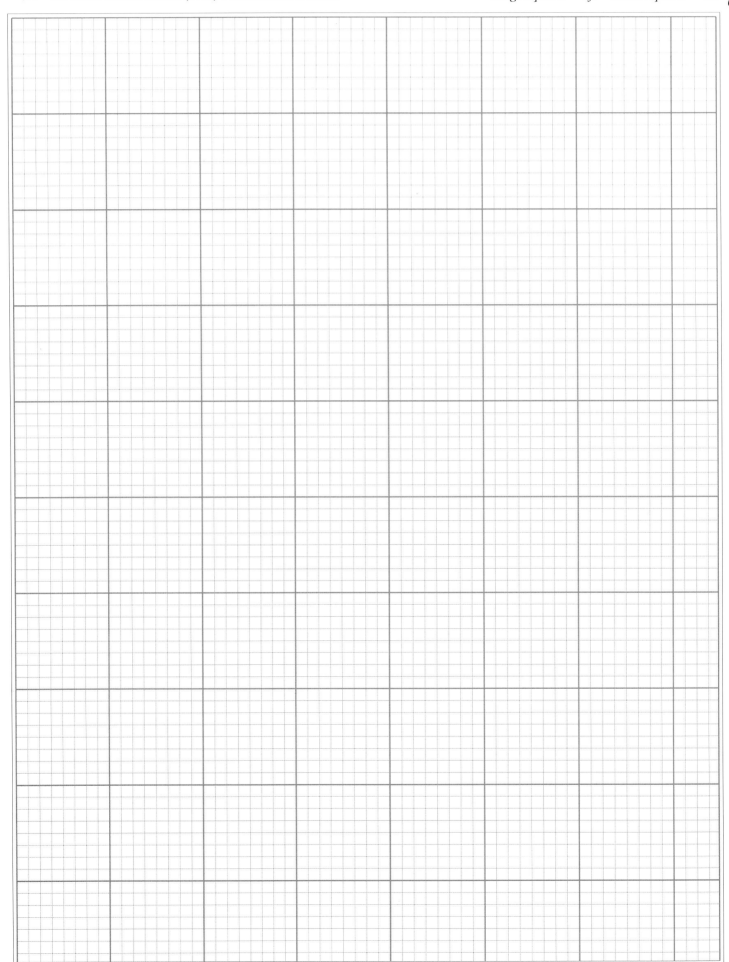